Palgrave Studies in the Economic Thou

CW00840221

Series editors

Avi Cohen
York University and University of Toronto
Toronto, Canada

G.C. Harcourt
University of New South Wales
Sydney, New South Wales, Australia

Peter Kriesler
University of New South Wales
Sydney, New South Wales, Australia

Jan Toporowski
School of Oriental and African Studies
London, United Kingdom

"Max's determination to get to the bottom of any problem he confronts and then explain how to think about it, rigorously and clearly, is the fruit of a profound diligence – an absolute refusal to be sloppy, confused or misleading. This diligence made him the remarkable teacher and analyst he is."
—Martin Wolf, Chief Economics Commentator, *Financial Times*

Palgrave Studies in the History of Economic Thought publishes contributions by leading scholars, illuminating key events, theories and individuals that have had a lasting impact on the development of modern-day economics. The topics covered include the development of economies, institutions and theories.

More information about this series at
http://www.palgrave.com/gp/series/14585

"A running theme of this book which has great contemporary resonance in many countries is Corden's reflections on what it means to be an immigrant. He reflects on the challenges facing newly-arrived immigrants, how they seek to assimilate to the receiving country's culture and values and how public policy can best facilitate this process. He draws heavily on his own family experience as refugees to Australia fleeing Nazi persecution. How does it affect the sense of identity? In his case he was much influenced, especially during the War, by Australia's British culture and education. Politicians and the media who wax glibly about immigration and assimilation would benefit greatly from reading this book."

—John Martin, former OECD Director for Employment,
Labour and Social Affairs, and current adviser to the
Irish government on employment policy

Warner Max Corden

Lucky Boy in the Lucky Country

The Autobiography of Max Corden, Economist

to Jane, with love from
Max
In Memors of John

palgrave
macmillan

Warner Max Corden
University of Melbourne
Melbourne, VIC, Australia
http://www.maxcorden.com

Palgrave Studies in the History of Economic Thought
ISBN 978-3-319-65165-1   ISBN 978-3-319-65166-8   (eBook)
DOI 10.1007/978-3-319-65166-8

Library of Congress Control Number: 2017954309

Cover illustration: author's own

Printed on acid-free paper

This Palgrave Macmillan imprint is published by Springer Nature
The registered company is Springer International Publishing AG
The registered company address is: Gewerbestrasse 11, 6330 Cham, Switzerland

To the memory of ...
Dorothy
My parents, Kate and Rudolf Corden
My brother, Gerald
Aunt Elli
Uncle Willy
Harry Johnson

Thank You

Thank You

Alex Millmow
Belinda Nemec
Daryl Stevens
Francesco Mongelli
Joe Isaac
John Creedy
John Nieuwenhuysen
Jonathan Thong
Hal Hill
Henryk Kierzkowski
Peter Dixon
Philip O'Brien
Prema-Chandra Athukorala
Rick Batzdorf
Sisira Jayasuriya
Sarath Rajapatirana
Tamar Gazit

And Especial Thanks To

Norbert Conrads
Geoff Harcourt
John Martin
John Black
Peter Oppenheimer
Ross Garnaut

Foreword by Martin Wolf

Max Corden—then, as he tells us, Werner Max Cohn—was born in Breslau in 1927 and moved to England in 1938. A lifelong Anglophile, he left for Australia with his family in 1939. There he was to become what he is today: Max Corden, Australia's greatest living economist. This book tells his remarkable story.

I first met Max during his period teaching at Nuffield College, Oxford, between 1967 and 1976. I was a student at Nuffield between 1969 and 1971 and was one of those people lucky enough to learn international trade theory from Max, who was not only one of the world's leading specialists but also a superb teacher.

The characteristics of Max as a teacher are the same as those of Max as an author—indeed they are very much on display in this autobiography: the maximum of clarity with the minimum of unnecessary complexity. I consider of this lack of pretension as an Australian virtue. But it went with a commitment to ideas that is characteristically Jewish.

Max was far and away the best teacher and most lucid expositor I met during my time at Oxford. I think of those qualities as not just intellectual—though, of course, they are—but also moral.

Max's determination to get to the bottom of any problem he confronts and then explain how to think about it, rigorously and clearly, is the fruit of a profound diligence—an absolute refusal to be sloppy, confused, or misleading. This diligence made him the remarkable teacher and analyst he is. And this, more than any particular bit of economics, was the most important lesson he imparted to me. He is an outstanding teacher and economist, because he is determined to perform his tasks to the very best of his abilities.

I drew two more lessons of great importance from Max. Since my background at Oxford had been in classics and then Politics, Philosophy, and Economics, I lacked the mathematical skills that were increasingly in demand. As a result, I wondered whether I could find my own niche in economics. Max, who eschewed mathematics in his theoretical work, showed me that I could hope to do so. Economics, it was clear, had many houses. In one of them I could hope to thrive.

The second lesson was his ability to underline something I already believed. Economics was a political subject. Its proper aim was to make the world a better place. With his deep interest in practical questions, Max taught me that this was an altogether reasonable ambition. He also taught me something else: as he puts it in the book, "one's choice of models must depend on circumstances". Economics is not a religion; it is a toolbox.

At the time I met him, Max was in the middle of what was arguably his most intellectually creative period, when he did his seminal work on protection and trade policy. The interest in trade I learned from him has stayed with me ever since. His book, *Trade Policy and Economic Welfare*, published in 1974, shortly after I left Oxford is, I believe, his masterpiece. It has had a huge influence upon me and many others.

Subsequently, Max moved to work on problems of the international monetary system. In this area, too, his writings were marked by those characteristics of clarity and rigour. He sorted things out and so, when one read his work, one learned how to understand the issues, too.

In this fascinating book, Max tells of his entire life journey, starting with Breslau, the arrival of the Nazi in 1933 and his father's imprisonment in Buchenwald, to the family's very lucky escape to England and then Australia. He puzzles, rightly over the mystery of the demented and murderous anti-Semitism he managed to escape.

Max goes on to explain how he became who he is—an Australian and a great economist. Here, too, he enjoyed much luck. As is usually the case, great success requires the timely help of a number of kind and decent people. Max received this. And he repaid this help, over and again, to his country and the world.

In a sane world, Max would now be a celebrated German scholar. As it is, he was indeed lucky to survive the wreck of the twentieth-century Europe. But his new country was lucky, too. By virtue of its far-sighted generosity, Australia gained an economist who contributed vastly to the domestic policy debate and added to his country's global reputation. And I, as a result, gained my foremost teacher and a lifelong friend.

Chief Economics Commentator, *Financial Times*   Martin Wolf

Contents

Part I

The Early Years

1

Breslau Boy

A Journey to England

On 19 April 1938 at the Breslau railway station, a small boy with coal-black curly hair arrived with a lady, presumably his mother. He was ten years old, though he probably looked younger. It was in the afternoon. He was carrying a raincoat over his arm and a small case. His mother, who seemed a bit weepy, told him not to lose the raincoat and case, and to remember two words, namely "Thank you" and *Danke Schön*, which means "Thank you" in German. He took up his seat in the train to Berlin. Of course he was alone. The trip lasted about five hours. At the Berlin railway station, he got out with his coat and case and met his Aunt Siddy, who brought him to her home by taxi. There he met his cousin, Peter, who was nine years old, and they all had supper together. But then something strange happened. Peter just disappeared!

After supper Aunt Siddy took the little boy into their living room, where she had made up a bed for him on a big couch. He took his pyjamas from his case and got dressed for going to bed. And Aunt Siddy pulled the curtains together and the room was dark, ready for his sleep. Then she left the room.

© The Author(s) 2017
W.M. Corden, *Lucky Boy in the Lucky Country*, Palgrave Studies in the History of Economic Thought, DOI 10.1007/978-3-319-65166-8_1

And then, something quite extraordinary happened, never to be forgotten by the little boy and his cousin, even when they were both over 80 years old. Peter emerged from underneath the couch. All this time he had been hiding there.

That was the end of the first day.

The next day, in the evening, Aunt Siddy took the little boy to the Berlin Railway station and put him on a train that was going to Holland, right across Germany to the West. He would travel with an elderly gentleman, probably Jewish, whom he had never met before. Even now, he does not know who he was. As the train left Berlin station and the little boy looked back, he could see the fireworks in Berlin. That would have been because of celebrations since 20th April was Hitler's birthday.

At the border between Germany and Holland some very nice Dutch officials came by and looked at passports. What a pleasure to meet some nice officials! Then the train went on to Hook van Holland, the port from where boats went to Harwich, England.

When and where did the little boy sleep? I don't know. I don't think he slept on the boat. But he remembers walking on the deck early in the morning. But there was something he does remember. He was always drawing, and he had coloured pencils and paper in his case. What he could see in front of him was the sea, but that is not what he was drawing. He was drawing a scene of mountains, and a winding mountain foot-path, and a little house. That was odd, considering what he was seeing. Two English ladies (elderly, perhaps 40) were very surprised and asked him. In a letter to his parents, he claimed later that they had had a conversation, which his parents thought improbable when his only English was "Thank you". But why was he drawing a mountain scene while looking at water? Years later, he was able to explain it. His mother had taken him on a holiday for just the two of them shortly before he left for England, and that was in the beautiful mountain country near Breslau— das *Riesengebirge* (Giant Mountains)—close to the Czech border, and it is a holiday he has never forgotten.

The end of this short story is that at Harwich, in England, he took a train to London, still with the unknown gentleman, and at Liverpool Street Station Aunt Elli was waiting for him. She took him by taxi to her small terrace house in Blenheim Terrace, St John's Wood, where he met his Uncle Henry and, more important, their dog, Jacky. He was then allowed to take Jacky for a walk to the end of the street, where it met the main road (Abbey Road).

This Was Me!

Of course, that little boy with curly black hair was me. My name was Werner Max Cohn. Werner is a common German name, but I don't know why that was chosen. Max was the name commonly used for my maternal grandfather, though his actual first name was Matthias.

I was born on 13 August 1927 in Breslau, the second largest city in Prussia and the eighth largest in Germany at the time. It was the capital of the province of Silesia. At that time, the population of Breslau was about 600,000, of which roughly 24,000 were Jews. The Jewish community of Breslau was the third largest in Germany, after Berlin and Frankfurt.

From Bohemia to the Weimar Republic

Breslau has a complex history as the capital of the province of Silesia but under varying names as the province has had changing overlords. From 1335, it was a part of the Kingdom of Bohemia until 1526 when it came to be ruled by the Habsburg Monarchy (i.e. the Austro-Hungarian Empire). In 1741, after the Seven Years War, Frederick the Great acquired it for Prussia from Maria Theresa. Subsequently in 1871, it became a part of the new German Empire, in which Prussia was the most important component. Throughout this time, the population of Breslau was (like my family) German speaking.

From 1918, the Kaiser's Empire was replaced by the Weimar Republic, which was destroyed by Hitler's Nazis in 1933. And that is where my story really begins.

But the story of Breslau does not end there: In 1945, Hitler's Germany lost the Second World War and thus also lost Silesia to Poland. So now Breslau has the new Polish name of *Wroclaw*. For further details on all this, see Davies and Moorhouse's *Microcosm: Portrait of a Central European City.*

The year of my birth, 1927, was the time of the (democratic) Weimar Republic, after the great inflation of 1923 and six years before the Nazi takeover of 1933, when Adolf Hitler became Chancellor. Hence, it was a brief period of reasonable stability in Germany.

My Father, My Mother, and My Brother

My father, Rudolf Simon Cohn, had served in the Great War (he was 18 years old in 1914) and afterwards attended the University of Breslau and obtained a law degree. My mother, Kate Sophie Levy, also attended the university and studied English and French. She was 19 when they married in 1920. She did not complete her degree. As the names Cohn and Levy indicate, they were both Jewish.

My only brother, Gerhart Martin Cohn, was born in 1922. The name Gerhart was very popular in Silesia at the time because a local boy, Gerhart Hauptmann, poet and playwright, had won the Nobel Prize for literature. Martin was the name of Rudolf's oldest brother who died unexpectedly in the same year at the age of 49. He was a railway engineer—and Gerhart also eventually became an engineer.

Louis Cohn from Provinz Posen

My father's father, Louis Cohn, was born in Provinz Posen, and at the age of 14, in 1857, came to Breslau, a flourishing city at that time, as indeed later. Posen was a province of Prussia, just like Silesia. Many years earlier, it had been a part of the country of Poland, but the latter was then split between Prussia, Russia, and Austria-Hungary. Its population consisted mostly of Poles and also of a considerable number of Jews—the Poles having been the farmers and the Jews the traders. Like many of his fellow Jews, Louis came from a very small town (Samter) and was fairly orthodox in his religious beliefs and practices, though he did go to a Reform synagogue in Breslau. His mother's maiden name was Hollander, and this gives an indication of the origin of her family. Her grandfather was a rabbi named Scholaum Amsterdam. It is well-known that many Sephardic Jews (refugees from Spain in 1492) went to the Netherlands, and, many years ago, many Jews went from western Germany (the Rhineland) and the Netherlands to Poland, bringing with them the Yiddish language, a medieval version of German.

A Flourishing Business in Breslau

When Louis went to Breslau in 1857, he was accompanied by his brother Moritz. Together, and with the help of funds from their sister, they purchased the business of two ladies with the surname of Trautner. This business was in *Posamenten*, which is often translated as "trimmings" but might possibly be described as haberdashery. It was located in a side street, running off The Ring (central square) of Breslau. Later they moved to Ring 52, and in 1902 purchased Ring 49 and had built in the latest Art Nouveau style a fine new building. This building was not damaged at the end of the Second World War; hence, it can still be seen.

The whole building was owned by the Cohn family, and the lower two stories were occupied by the family firm *Geschwister Trautner Nachfolger*. (This means the successors of the Trautner sisters.) That northern side of the Ring came to be known popularly as the Trautner side. Louis, presumably with the support of his brother, Moritz, devoted himself to building up and managing this firm. He died unexpectedly early at the age of 60 in 1903, and thus was hardly able to enjoy his success. But he had laid the foundation for the considerable success of the Cohn family. He had himself become a highly respected citizen of Breslau, and he was an active member of the Jewish community.

Briefly, the subsequent history of Trautner was as follows. Louis had six surviving children, five boys and one girl. (See the Cohn family tree on page 8.) After his first wife died, he married Margarethe Hainauer, mother of the youngest three, namely Willy, Erna, and Rudolf (my father). Martin was the oldest, an engineer, whom I have already mentioned. The second was Hugo, who succeeded his father in the management of Trautner. He managed the firm jointly with his uncle Moritz, brother of Louis. In 1939, Moritz emigrated with his family to South America. Hugo died in 1932, and then my father, Rudolf, the youngest son of Louis, took over. But it seems that in the same year, or possibly even earlier, the firm had got into financial difficulties. This was most likely an effect of the Great Depression which hit the German economy particularly hard. So the firm was sold to a Jewish businessman, but Rudolf stayed as manager, and this is the role in which I remember my father vividly. At this stage, the ownership of the Ring 49 building (as distinct from the Trautner firm) stayed with the family.

COHN FAMILY TREE

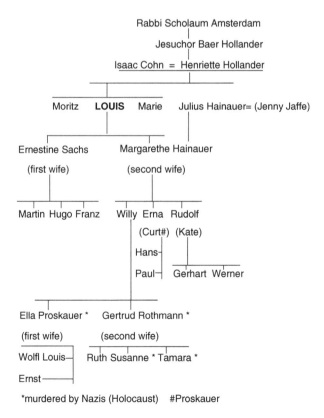

*murdered by Nazis (Holocaust)   #Proskauer

Please note that in the family tree, the three oldest sons of Louis, namely Martin, Hugo, and Franz, all died before the first impact of the Nazi take-over in 1937 (dates of death: 1922, 1932, and 1934 respectively).

My Father Becomes Unemployed

In 1937, the Nazi regime commenced the process of *Arisierung*: only an "Aryan" (non-Jew) could manage other Aryans. Therefore, my father was dismissed as manager of Trautner. Some person named Paul Grzesik took over in 1938. My father, thus, became unemployed. I am sure that was decisive: the family had to emigrate. In retrospect, that decision was the best thing that could have happened. In July 1939, the remaining member of the family, Willy, the fourth son of Louis—about whom I shall be writing much more—sold the Ring 49 building, no doubt under pressure, to the same Grzesik.

Aunt Elli and Aunt Siddy

I have already mentioned my mother's two sisters, namely Aunt Elli and Aunt Siddy.

Until 1933, Aunt Elli and her husband Heinrich had lived in Berlin. When Hitler became Chancellor of Germany in 1933, Heinrich had the wisdom to decide that Germany was no longer a country he wanted to live in. That was incredibly sensible and turned out very important for thewholefamily,includingGerhartandme. So, HeinrichandElliimmigrated to England and lived in London. Heinrich changed his name to Henry. Siddy and her family, including son Peter, also lived in Berlin, but emigrated at a very late stage.

Emigration: Gerhart and Werner Emigrate

My brother Gerhart, aged 15, was sent to England in 1937 and attended school there—The Royal Grammar School in High Wycombe—until late 1938. I, Werner, aged 10, was sent in April 1938 to a preparatory

("Prep") school in Westgate-on-Sea, Kent, where I too stayed until late 1938. All this was arranged by Aunt Elli. I think that generous British donors would have paid our school fees.

Both Gerhart and I stayed for a short time with Elli and Henry in London before being taken to our schools. I am sure that Elli would also have persuaded my parents that there was no alternative to all four of us getting out of Germany.

Of course, visas had to be obtained. Britain had special refugee visas for children. Crucial for the whole family eventually were the visas for Australia. I believe we also owe these to Aunt Elli. I am sure these were much easier to obtain from London than from a provincial German city. At an international conference at Evian in Switzerland, various countries had agreed to take a limited number of German (and Austrian) Jewish refugees. Australia had agreed to a quota of 5000 for the first year. I wonder how we four managed to get into this lucky group when there must have been about 600,000 Jews from Germany and Austria wanting desperately to get out of a country that for many years they thought they belonged to. One thing I do know: we owe the quota to some sympathetic Australian politicians. And we also owe a great deal to the British, who provided special visas for child refugees.

Kristallnacht: Father Taken to Buchenwald

Kristallnacht happened on 9 November 1938. (Roughly translated, this means "Night of Broken Glass".) This was a historic night of infamy. For a full explanation and description see chapter 4 of Ascher, *A Community Under Siege*. It was an explosion of Nazi hate against Jews all over Germany, including Breslau. Nationally, the Nazis arrested about 30,000 males, and my father was one of them. They were sent to concentration camps—Dachau, Buchenwald, or Sachsenhausen. My father was sent to Buchenwald. About 1400 synagogues were set on fire in Germany, including Breslau's New Synagogue. Jewish-owned shops had their windows broken. There was massive looting. Jewish assets were seized. One victim of Buchenwald has reported "the sadism of the guards, their delight in humiliating the prisoners" (Ascher, p. 185).

My father was simply picked up in the street, and he disappeared. My mother had to go to the Gestapo many times to find out where he was. All this was happening while Gerhart and I were in school in England and knew nothing about it. Reflecting on this, it seems to me that these events would have been reported in British newspapers, and probably our school headmasters ensured that we did not know about them.

The policy of the Nazis at that time was that they wanted Jews to emigrate as fast as possible to make Germany *Judenrein* (completely free of Jews). Many prisoners in the concentration camps did die, but killing was not yet systematic. Thus, they were willing to release a prisoner if there was proof that he and his family had visas to go abroad. It was fortunate that the process of getting a visa to go to Australia had been initiated by my parents before Kristallnacht, of course with the crucial help of Aunt Elli. The effort was motivated not only by the fact that my father had lost his job in 1937 but also by the gradual realisation of the deteriorating situation of Jews in Germany.

Buchenwald was the concentration camp very close to Weimar. My father was there for 16 days. He never described his experience to me or Gerhart, and we did not ask. He was let out from Buchenwald once my mother was able to show the Gestapo that she had a visa for him and herself to go to Australia.

My Father Comes Back from Buchenwald

What happened next? Only recently, in December 2016, I found out from a memoir that my mother had written what happened when my father returned to Breslau from Buchenwald. Apparently, he was "in a terrible state" and was warned by the Gestapo that they will want him back again unless he went abroad straight away. So, immediately he flew to England without my mother, staying, I assume, with Henry and Elli. But my mother had yet to get a passport and could not leave with him. After a few weeks, she got her passport and followed him to England, whether flying or by train and ship, I do not know. So, now, we two boys and our parents were in England.

On 16 December 1938, we were all in Southampton, off to Australia on a Rotterdamsche Lloyd ship, the MS *Sibayak*, with Aunt Elli waving us goodbye.

A friend who has read what I have written above asked me: Why, in later, happier years in Melbourne, did my brother and I not ask my father about Buchenwald? Here is my answer. There were lots of things that my parents did not want to talk about; they wanted to leave behind unpleasant things of the past. I sensed that. Remember that the Nazis, above all, wanted to *humiliate* people—that is, Jews and political enemies. It was the best way of making them suffer. To go into a concentration camp was not like being a hero in a war; you were made aware that you were *scum*. You did not feel like a hero. The unfortunate thing about people like my father was that they were not proud of being Jewish. They wanted to be German. This was different from Uncle Willy, about whom I write in Chap. 3.

Breslau Under the Nazis

Terrible things happened in Breslau, as indeed elsewhere in Germany, when Hitler became Chancellor in 1933, and effectively the Nazis destroyed the democratic Weimar Republic and pursued a reign of terror first against their political enemies—the social democrats and the communists—and then the Jews.

I turned six in 1933 and was too young to understand what was going on. Hence, I will just give here a few recollections of my peaceful and innocent life. Actually, it was a nightmare, though not for me. There is a full and indeed brilliant account of Breslau before and under the Nazis in one chapter of Davies and Moorhouse's *Microcosm: Portrait of a Central European City*. For me, reading this chapter is just a reminder of how lucky the Cohn boys had been.

If I look back on the five years—from 1933 to 1937—when I lived in Breslau under the Nazis between my ages of six and ten, I must say that Nazi thinking and events played a very small role in my life. Above all, my parents sheltered me from the awareness of crisis, especially in 1937, when my father lost his job and Gerhart left for England. Even in 1938, when I was put on a train to Berlin, as the first stage of my journey to England, I was not really worried or upset. All that I remember is my concern not to lose the small suitcase I was carrying and the coat over my arm.

My Comfortable Middle-Class Breslau Life

For the whole period, including the years before 1933, my life in Breslau was dominated by two activities, namely ice-skating in winter and visits to the *Süd-Park* (South Park) in summer. These are also my predominant memories. In winter, tennis courts would be frozen, and that is where one skated. In summer, I went with my mother to a beautiful park in the south of Breslau, a longish walk from our home. I note that this park was originally designed by the botanist Professor Ferdinand Julius Cohn (known as the father of bacteriology). He was no relative but, of course, a Jew. We walked in the park and sat on park benches. (Later, after we left Breslau, Uncle Willy has recorded that there were notices that Jews must not sit on these benches.) In the park was a wonderful, memorable lake which usually froze in winter, and I skated there too. Indeed, that was a highlight.

But there was more of a comfortable middle-class life—including going to the cinema to see films of Shirley Temple (and newsreels with Adolf Hitler), learning to swim, playing with toy soldiers in German uniform, and so on. I also recall frequently buying a newspaper for the family at the street corner of Menzel and Kaiser Wilhelm Strasse and reading it on the way back. For some reason, I always remember the headline "Eden Resigns". And I read or browsed among my parents' books. All quite mundane. I had several friends, all Jewish, and relatively little contact with Gerhart because he was five years older than me. And there were regular visits to *Grossmutti* Cohn (who had sweets waiting for me).

There were also visits to Trautner and to the Jewish-owned department store Wertheim, where a friend of the family worked as a junior manager and where one could buy mouth-watering *belegte Broetchen* from a machine. (These were small open sandwiches with meat and cheese.)

I certainly remember going to synagogue, but that was not frequent. I do recall one *Seder* (Passover ceremony) with the family of Uncle Herbert, my mother's brother, at their home. I had the important role of asking (in Hebrew) the questions that fall to the youngest participant: Why is this day different from all other days? As far as I remember, my father knew no Hebrew and had little interest in religious occasions. The presiding role at the *Seder* (answering my questions) was played by Uncle Jena, the father-in-law of Uncle Herbert.

On the matter of religion, and my father's inadequacy on this matter expressed publicly, I must record the following. Uncle Willy—who was seriously religious and hence observant—kept a diary which was published post-war (well after he was murdered). He recorded that on 23 January 1937, he had Gerhart and me to supper. He apparently wanted to check up whether my father was bringing us up properly with respect to Judaism. I quote from the English translation of the diary: "The younger one in particular (that was me!) has a certain feel for what it means to be Jewish; perhaps he is compensating for the sins of his father against Judaism!"

What do I recall about events related to the 1933 Nazi takeover? I was impressed by groups of soldiers or brown-shirts (SA men) marching, while singing, in the street. I found that thrilling and probably would have wanted to join them. I noted display boxes, especially in the main boulevard, the Kaiser Wilhelm Strasse, showing the front page of the *Der Stuermer* newspaper with pictures or sketches of ugly big-nosed Jews and anti-Semitic messages. This especially unpleasant Nazi newspaper possibly did not sell well, so these display boxes were meant to broaden its readership. Of course, I stopped and read it if my parents were not with me. I was thinking: my father is not like that.

Until 1935, I and other Jewish children went to a state (government) school, and I do not have any unpleasant memories. At the end of 1935, all Jewish children had to leave these schools and go to special Jewish schools. I recall the last day when the parents came to a farewell function, and my teacher, whom I liked very much, said how sorry he was that we had to leave. When my parents got home, my father remarked that this teacher (Herr Blumel) had a Nazi membership badge on his lapel.

I vividly recall a visit to my hairdresser not long before I left for England, with him saying to me, "Sit still, Jewboy". More significant was a memory of Gerhart's, whose Breslau experiences were that of a teenager. He told me later (in Melbourne) that if he saw a group of boys in the street, he would always go to the other side to avoid them. Of course, in Melbourne that was not necessary.

Yes, I Saw Hitler

And then, there is the day I saw Hitler. It was 1937. Unforgettable! He had visited Breslau and made a speech to a big crowd at Breslau's famous *Jahrhunderthalle* (centenary hall). Afterwards he was driven in his black Mercedes to the south, along Kaiser Wilhelm Strasse, to the airport. We lived close to this grand boulevard. The street was lined with police or brown-shirts and crowds. The General Post Office, also near us, faced this street. Jews, of course, were not meant to be visible at such occasions. I think I remember that I (aged nine) sneaked out, without the knowledge of my parents, joined the crowd in front of the General Post Office, and, being small, the police or SA men pushed me right in front. My memory is unclear on this crucial matter, but I think (and now confess) that I joined the crowd in giving the "Heil Hitler" salute as Hitler, in an open car, standing, came past. The plain fact is that I was thinking like a German—almost every German—with no awareness of the evil he was yet to do. As I write this, I wonder: did this really happen, or did I just dream it?

Bibliography

Ascher, Abraham (2007) *A Community Under Siege: The Jews of Breslau under Nazism.*

Davies, Norman and Roger Moorhouse (2002) Microcosm: *A Portrait of a Central European City,* Jonathan Cape, London.

2

Why Do They Hate Us So Much?

The central feature of my early life and its consequences was German anti-Semitism. Without such anti-Semitism, we would never have left Germany for Australia. I have never ceased being aware of our luck in getting out in time. And even though I left so early in life—and have never personally suffered as so many others have – the experience has affected me permanently. The Holocaust and paranoia are always there. Therefore, I greatly welcomed a book I discovered recently which thoroughly analyses the big question. Its title poses the issue: *Why the Germans? Why the Jews?* Götz Aly (2014). The author is a German historian. A large part of my chapter here draws on this book. His main point, supported by much evidence, is that anti-Semitism was already strong in Germany in the nineteenth century, well before Hitler.

But Stop! Stop! This is an autobiography you are writing, and not a book of history. You have left your family in Southampton while waiting to take the ship to Australia. Yes, but this history is, indeed, important because it is about the deep background to what happened to my family, kicked out of our country for no good reason. Or, if there is a good reason, there is a need to study it.

It is well known that anti-Semitism in Europe has a long history and has certainly not been unique to Germany. For many years in many

© The Author(s) 2017
W.M. Corden, *Lucky Boy in the Lucky Country*, Palgrave Studies in the History of Economic Thought, DOI 10.1007/978-3-319-65166-8_2

countries, the motive was essentially religious, as can be seen most clearly in the Spanish case, where the ascendency of Catholic rulers brought about the mass expulsion of Jews from Spain in 1492. Earlier, the Crusades also led to the persecution of Jews, again motivated by religion. Jews lived in ghettos not because of their choice but because of restrictions imposed by rulers. And they engaged in limited activities, notably trading and money-lending, because of restrictions, such as on owning land, engaging in agriculture, or joining the military, and so on. But what kept them going and united was their religion and especially the study (obsessive, I would say) of their religious literature—the Torah.

The religious motive for anti-Semitism weakened with the Enlightenment (which began in France in the second half of the eighteenth century) and a new, uniquely German motive developed, namely the focus on "race." The view became prevalent in Germany that the Jews were a distinct and undesirable race, inferior to the very superior German race. Religious anti-Semitism went into the background (though not disappearing), so that Jews could not avoid anti-Semitism by converting to Christianity.

The Green-Eyed Monster

Götz Aly shows in detail that anti-Semitism in Germany in this new form was popular and widespread at least from the beginning of the nineteenth century. Thus its roots go deep, well before Hitler. It went right through the society, from the low-educated "masses" to many intellectuals. Essentially it was caused by two intersecting factors, namely the economic transition in Germany and the Jewish emancipation.

Germany, like Britain, or perhaps following it, had an industrial revolution associated with an agricultural revolution, which led to a mass movement of people out of agriculture into industry and out of villages and small towns into cities. Some cities, notably Berlin, became very large. This was also associated with a financial revolution and with many changes, such as the development of large retail department stores competing with small shops. A new, specialised professional class grew up—doctors, lawyers, and so on. In addition, more under the influence of the

Enlightenment (which might be described as a rebellion against the dominance of the churches), there was an educational revolution. New, modern universities were established. All this upset a conservative, initially small-town and village, population. There were gainers and losers, and the losers were not happy. In fact, many people hated all these changes.

The other development was the emancipation of the Jews, definitely a major event in modern Jewish history. Jews were liberated from the tight restrictions of the ghetto imposed on them by the rulers. They became free to enter German society. To a varying extent, they were given rights of citizenship. This all took place under the influence of the French Enlightenment, mostly imposed by Napoleon on Germany when he controlled much of Germany. It was also favoured by some parts of the German ruling class.

Division among the Jews emerged. There were those who adhered to their language, their Orthodox religion, their very rigid customs, and their rabbis and thus continued their ghetto life, but in self-isolation. But others wanted to seize the new opportunities. They were mostly the young. They learned to speak and write in German if they did not do so already, they dressed like respectable middle-class Germans, and they flooded the advanced schools and the universities. They entered German politics. They became, what we now call, assimilated Jews—in practice the antecedents of people like my family. And they were highly successful. Jews may only have been 1% of the population, but they would have been (say) 10% of the university students. Götz Aly describes this development in detail.

Jews now provided competition, or at least unwelcome role models, for many Germans. Many of these Jews were much more literate than the German population. Years of study and debate about the Torah had prepared them for intellectual activity and scientific thinking. Above all, they were more prepared for urban, big-city working and living. This led to deep jealousy—what Shakespeare in Othello called "The Green-Eyed Monster" – felt both by the masses and at least some of the intellectuals and artists for whom Jews also provided competition. Here, perhaps the best example is Richard Wagner, who hated Jewish composers.

The success of some Jews was indeed remarkable. They were high achievers. Because of their success and apparent acceptance by the German population, or at least its ruling classes, one might have thought that the Jews in the nineteenth century were better off in Germany than in any other European country. After all, leading writers and politicians were Jewish. Bismarck had Jewish financiers to advise him, notably the famous Gerson Bleichroeder. It is true that England had Disraeli as Prime Minister, yet the number of prominent Jews was much greater in Germany. But they were hated for their success, as high achievers often are.

The success of the Jews in the modern economy developed a kind of inferiority complex among (some) Germans. It is here that the new emphasis on "race" compensated. This was well before Hitler. Germans were persuaded that they belonged to a superior "race", which was independent of exceptional success in various activities. Rather, the message was that Jews were inherently *inferior* and Germans inherently superior, not only to Jews but also, for example, to Slavs.

I am summarising here the arguments, supported with much more historical detail, by Götz Aly. In the early nineteenth century, Germans were, basically, an unhappy people, looking for an ideology that would give them confidence. Götz Aly makes two important points. One was that, unlike France and England, Germany was not a united nation. There were many kingdoms, duchies, and principalities that were endlessly squabbling among themselves. Unity came only in 1871, under the leadership of Prussia. The idea of "race" gave a sense of unity. The other point made by Götz Aly was that Germany had been an occupied country, occupied by Napoleon, with thousands of young Germans conscripted, and many, young and old, killed. They hated the French, and the emancipation of the German Jews was identified with French rule. In addition, he mentions that the Thirty Years' War from 1618 to 1648 between Catholics and Protestants had been effectively a disastrous German civil war, also reducing German power and pride.

Heinrich Heine, an Assimilated Jew

One outstanding figure of an assimilated Jew was Heinrich Heine. He has been one of Germany's greatest poets, much quoted. One of his most famous poems, based on a Rhineland myth, was *Die Lorelei*. I don't know whether it is still true, but there was a time when every German child learned it at school. I can still recite it in perfect German (if only to demonstrate my mastery of the language!). It has been set to music by Schubert.

My father's favourite quotation of Heine's was *Denk ich an Deutschland in der Nacht dann bin ich um den Schlaf gebracht* (When I think of Germany at night, then I lose my sleep). Heine was also an essayist and a frank critic of German politics. Amazingly, while he always wrote in German, and published in Germany, in the latter part of his life he chose to live in Paris, essentially because he was sick of always being labelled as a Jewish poet (rather than a German one) in Germany.

Anti-Semitism and the Politics of Cultural Despair

Much has been written about the history of anti-Semitism in Germany both in the nineteenth and the early twentieth century. I have found two exceptionally useful books, both impressive works of scholarship, namely Fritz Stern's *The Politics of Cultural Despair* and Peter Pulzer's *The Rise of Political Anti-Semitism in Germany and Austria*. These fill out in detail the picture painted by Götz Aly.

The transformation of Germany during the nineteenth century was associated with what was then called liberalism. This ideology was imported from Britain, but it also had elements of the French Enlightenment. This coincided with the industrial revolution, and hence the decline of agriculture. By the end of the nineteenth century, Germany—now united under Prussian leadership—was a major industrial power. There was an emphasis on materialism, on parliamentary (multiparty) democracy, on free speech, and on what was called "Manchesterism" or what we now call the free market ideology. Perhaps one can sum it all up as modernism. This was hated by some conservative intellectuals, who wanted to recapture an idealised past, and their views were widely shared. In their eyes (to quote Stern), "The Jew was the very incarnation of modernity". It was this dislike of change that dominated a large part of society and stimulated anti-Semitism. Stern describes in detail the ideas and the influence of Paul de Lagarde, whose writings for many years had a big influence, notably on the Nazis. The enemy was liberalism and all those who prospered under it, notably the Jews.

People resented Jews not only because they were jealous of the Jews' success but also because they disliked the new secular culture in which Jews flourished. The so-called conservative cultural despair had extreme anti-Semitism as a by-product. They saw German nationalism as the alternative, and clearly Jews had no place in a nationalist ideal.

Anti-Semitism in the Twentieth Century

One can seemingly be brief about German anti-Semitism in the twentieth century. There were two causes for its sharp revival. The first was the loss in the First World War. Jews (like my father and his brother Willy) had fought in the Kaiser's army and made an effort to appear and be loyal Germans. Nevertheless, at the end Jews were blamed for the German defeat and its consequences. It was a defeat that the overconfident Germans had not expected. Of course, it must be the Jews! The second was the Great Depression, which led to massive unemployment and to the usual tendency to blame the Jews.

But how does this connect with popular German anti-Semitism, which has its roots in the nineteenth century and which I have explained at length as caused by the green-eyed monster? It is surely clear that the rise of Nazism, and hence Adolf Hitler, caused the Holocaust, but it is not at all obvious that this is connected with historic popular anti-Semitism.

At this point, I turn to another extremely informative book, namely Sarah Gordon's *Hitler, Germans, and the "Jewish Question"*. This is a book which is essentially about public opinion in Germany under Hitler. To what extent did the German people support or oppose Hitler, and to what extent were their attitudes towards Jews and Hitler influenced by historic anti-Semitism? I am thus exploring the connection between the issues discussed above by Götz Aly that concern popular anti-Semitism and the dreadful deeds of the Hitler regime. Could one find the roots of the Holocaust and its predecessors, notably Kristallnacht, in the nineteenth-century experience?

The German People and the Holocaust

There are some surprising facts that I learned from this book by Sarah Gordon.

1. The events of Kristallnacht were extraordinarily and almost universally unpopular in Germany from generals downward. This event offended against property rights (the sanctity of private property), the rule of law more generally, the whole idea of social order, and in addition made the persecution of Jews, with whom many sympathised, extremely visible. That taught Hitler a few lessons, notably that mis-treatment of Jews must not be visible or even known, to the public. I would add, as someone with German instincts, that there is nothing Germans want more than order and the rule of law. In addition, physi-cal violence and brutality were rejected by the majority.
2. Anti-Semitic propaganda was generally not popular, and notably, *Der Stuermer* (anti-Semitic Nazi newspaper) was disliked for being vulgar.
3. Rumours later about death camps and shootings in the east were apparently discounted as too fantastic to believe.
4. There is no indication that the anti-Semitic policy helped the Nazi party to get its large number of votes in 1933, and smaller parties with anti-Semitic platforms did not gain support at the crucial times. This does not rule out the high likelihood that there was a widespread degree of moderate anti-Semitism in 1933, as in earlier years.
5. The book by Gordon gives a full account of numerous cases of opposi-tion to Nazi policies and sympathy for Jews. These often required great courage and included Catholic and Protestant clergy. But there is no way of knowing how much support such opposition had, and indeed how the numbers compared with Nazi supporters, who were certain to be much more numerous. Any potential protester had to consider the likelihood of ending in a concentration camp.

One conclusion could be that the incredible extermination program was Hitler's personal programme based on an extraordinary ideology, which presumably had its roots in Hitler's personal experience or psy-chology. His supporters did not necessarily expect expulsion or extermination of Jews as a central policy of his regime. This book by Sarah Gordon describes his ideology in detail (Gordon 1984, pp. 91–117). Furthermore, it was not anti-Semitism that brought his party to power; rather it was the poor state of the economy combined with the disunity of the Opposition. Nevertheless, the existence of popular anti-Semitism—going back to the nineteenth century or earlier— made it much easier for Hitler to pursue his program. Furthermore, his success depended on the overemphasis by Germans (especially the military) on loyalty to a leader, however criminal or preposterous his ideology.

In my view, Hitler could not have achieved his murderous programme leading to the Holocaust without the active support of very many people, and, above all, without the willingness of many more Germans—notably military people—to shut their eyes to what was happening or to simply accept "realities". The question is what role historic anti-Semitism played in the outcome.

One must add here that, on the involvement of ordinary Germans in the Holocaust, one cannot ignore the historic case study reported in the classic book by Christopher Browning: *Ordinary Men: Reserve Police Battalion 101 and the Final Solution in Poland* (1992). A group of 500 "ordinary" men, recruited in Hamburg for the final solution in Poland, shot in the back of the neck, one by one 38,000 Jewish men, women, and children. These murderers were Hamburg citizens too old for the regular army. And there is more, but I need not elaborate on it.

Reflections on the Green-Eyed Monster: Need for Discretion

We have here in the nineteenth-century German experience and after a situation in which high achievers created benefits not just for themselves but also for others in the community, perhaps their customers or clients. This seems to be relevant to the Jewish experience in Germany before Hitler.

In Chap.1, I mentioned the pleasure that I derived by visiting the big department store in Breslau, called the Wertheim (named after the family that founded the chain). Indeed, it was usually crowded and very popular. Many German cities had such a store (and more than one in Berlin), and they were well patronised and usually all owned by Jews. This was one of the prominent contributions of Jews to German society. Such stores gave many Germans much pleasure. Yet anti-Semites complained, as if Jews had stolen these stores. Would they have preferred that they had never been invented?

Consider another case. Many medical doctors were Jewish, far more as a proportion of all doctors than were Jews in the population. Thus, there must have been many non-Jewish (Aryan) Germans who had Jewish doctors. They would have made a free choice perhaps because they thought that Jews were better doctors. Again, high achievers! When they saw their doctors being dragged away or insulted, did they not feel uneasy about anti-Semitism? That, indeed, seems likely.

Given what has happened to German Jews, is there a lesson here for high achievers? In some activities, Jews in Germany, on the average, were exceptionally successful, more so than the average German, and sometimes more even than the best non-Jewish Germans. This has been much studied and written about. And this kept the green-eyed monster busy. Should Jews have avoided these activities, and so avoided the monster? They did very well in studying medicine; should they have studied agriculture or perhaps sport instead? If they had bright new ideas in the area of business or finance, should they have pushed them to the back of their minds? The answers to these questions seem obvious. But I do think that there is a lesson which has been imprinted in the minds of assimilated German Jews: avoid the green-eyed monster, exercise discretion. This has certainly influenced me.

Bibliography

Aly, Götz, Why the Germans? Why the Jews? Envy, Race Hatred, and the Prehistory of the Holocaust, 2014
Gordon, Sarah, *Hitler, Germans, and the Jewish Question*, 1984
Pulzer, Peter, *The Rise of Political Anti-Semitism in Germany and Austria*, 1964
Stern, Fritz, *The Politics of Cultural Despair*, 1961
Goldfarb, Michael, *Emancipation: How Liberating Europe's Jews from the Ghetto led to Revolution and Renaissance*, 2009

3

Uncle Willy: The Jew Who Loved Germany

When I was a little boy in Breslau, my parents said that I was taking after Uncle Willy. That has stuck in my mind. I shall discuss later why this turned out to be only part true. But the story of Uncle Willy is, indeed, very important in any reflections on my life.

Uncle Willy was my father's older brother, born in 1888. (My father was born in 1896.) For 11 years, Willy was a high-school (or grammar school) teacher of history and German literature in Breslau. He was a very dedicated teacher, among other things, taking students for educational travels around Germany. He was dismissed from the school in 1933, when the Nazis came to power, because he was a committed and active social democrat. If that had not been a factor then, in due course, he would have been dismissed because he was a Jew. Because of his Jewishness, he never obtained a university position, even though he had a doctorate in history from the University of Breslau. After 1933, he taught history at the Jewish Theological Seminary in Breslau. In addition, he was a prolific writer and public lecturer.

He was a man of extraordinary energy and dedication. A list of his publications, both academic and journalistic, runs up to 491 items. Indeed, it is impossible to summarise it; it covered Jewish and German

© The Author(s) 2017
W.M. Corden, *Lucky Boy in the Lucky Country*, Palgrave Studies in the History of Economic Thought, DOI 10.1007/978-3-319-65166-8_3

history, current politics and social issues, and writings on medieval history. His speciality in the latter was the Normans in Sicily. The subject of his doctoral thesis was "The History of the Norman-Sicilian Fleet under the Rule of Rogers I and II". His particular interest in later years was the history of German Jews.

It is possible to know a great deal about Willy's life and ideas because he kept a diary all his life from a very early age to 1941, the year in which he was murdered, with full records of his activities and especially his thinking. On the basis of his diary, he dictated a massive autobiography not long before he died, and this fortunately survived his life and the war. It gives a full account of his activities and thinking up to 1933. In addition, there is his now-famous diary from 1933 to 1941, the period when he was living under the Nazi regime. We are indebted to Professor Norbert Conrads of Stuttgart University for the superb editing of both these works.

The War: 1914–1918

Willy's autobiography contains a substantial chapter describing his experience in the Kaiser's army during the First World War. He was a non-commissioned officer and earned the Iron Cross.

He has numerous war stories to tell. A special feature was that he was a rare German who was fluent in French. The German army was occupying a part of France and needed to communicate with the population. That was thus his special duty. He recalls one case where he had to convey to the extremely distraught population of an occupied French village that they all had to leave their homes and be transported elsewhere. While he was dictating this episode to his wife, he knew that exactly the same experience was happening to Jews in Nazi-occupied Europe and was likely to happen to him—which indeed it did.

In the Kaiser's army, he was determined always to do his duty and not evade difficult tasks; it was continually in his mind that he was a Jew and needed to show his fellow Germans that he was utterly brave and loyal. This colourful chapter of his autobiography is full of insights, which I cannot, unfortunately, summarise here. It is a pity that it has never been translated into English.

In the middle of his four-year service at the front, he was allowed to go on leave to Breslau. He describes the awkwardness of the experience. But he was delighted to meet his first son, Wolfgang Louis, who was born while he was at the front. He had been married in 1913. After the war, he had the familiar problem of veterans, being unable to adjust to society and renew a close relationship with his wife. They were divorced in 1922, and he married Gertrud (called Trudi) in 1923. He had two sons by Ella, his first wife, and three daughters by Gertrud.

The End

Unlike many German Jews at the time, and unlike my parents and their two sons, Willy never emigrated, though his three oldest children did. That left him, his second wife Gertrud, and two little girls. On 21 November 1941, all four of them were herded to an assembly camp in Breslau and eventually put on a train with a thousand Breslau Jews. Several days later, they arrived in Kaunas (Lithuania), where they were all murdered by a firing squad. Susanne was nine, and Tamara was three.

I shall discuss below—what has inevitably also been discussed by their surviving children: Why did they not emigrate and thus avoid this almost unbelievable fate?

No Justice in Germany: The Breslau Diaries 1933–1941

In Willy's book edited by Norbert Conrads, we get the details of an extraordinary period in the history of Breslau and Germany, in effect a case study of the gradual creation of Hell. What was it like being a Jew under the Nazi regime? These diaries have been published in two volumes adding up to 1000 pages. A condensed version in English, about 400 pages, is also available. The diaries have been cited and widely reviewed, and even referred to by the President of Germany in a notable speech.

An important question in the history of Germany is: How did the German people react to the Nazi persecution? It is clear that there were many active participants and very many nasty supporters, but there were also those who were passive onlookers or sympathisers with Jews. Willy has in his diaries many stories of sympathisers and even some whom I would call "exceptionally helpful". He refers to numerous individual encounters and describes the attitudes of the persons concerned.

With regard to Willy himself, he makes an effort to maintain his dignity. In reading his own account I think of the British term "stiff upper lip". It seems to help him that he is genuinely proud to be a Jew. This is a case where religious belief really helps.

Outstanding in the category of "exceptionally helpful" were the directors and staff of the archives and library of the Breslau Catholic Cathedral. Indeed, the diocese archives became his second home, especially for his absorbing research work on the *Germania Judaica* (history of the Jews in Germany), which began in June 1939 and went on until near the end of his life.

At that stage, he had already lost his teaching job. As part of the numerous obstacles put in the way of Jews by the Nazi regime, he was barred from using the city library and other libraries. Hence, the diocese archives were crucial for his scholarly work. He became good friends with the directors, Alfons Nowack (who died in 1939) and Kurt Engelbert, and especially with one distinguished Catholic scholar, Dr Hubert Jedin, who worked there. He was always warmly received, and if he did not turn up on any day, they worried about him. For him it was a place not just for research but for professional conversations, which he greatly appreciated.

Let me quote from his diary. "How happy I was to work once more in a scholarly setting." "This morning I was able to work undisturbed for several hours in the Diocese Archive, for which I am grateful every day. Doing this work I forget all my cares." "I really am extremely grateful for permission to work here." "Discussed a number of scholarly and other matters with Dr Jedin. He is of great help to me."

I find this very moving.

Later, when he expected he would have to leave Breslau and was concerned about the preservation of his diaries and autobiography, he arranged for one copy of all his note books (i.e. the diaries themselves and the autobiography dictated at the latest stage) to be deposited with their Berlin friend Paul Zeitz (a non-Jew who was married to a distant relative of Willy).

Why Did Willy Not Emigrate?

Some Jews did not manage to emigrate because they had not foreseen in time the crisis that was to come. But that was not the case of Willy. He, like most others, did not foresee organised mass murder. But surely, he would have foreseen increased pressure to emigrate or even actual physical expulsion. He was well aware of the great expulsion of Jews from Spain in 1492, which he saw as a parallel for current events. He was highly aware of the anti-Semitism in Germany when the 1914–1918 war was lost, and Jews were blamed. Being a German patriot and thus disappointed with this German reaction, he saw Zionism as the solution to the Jewish problem, one which involved the voluntary emigration of Jews from Germany. Indeed, he became a vigorous advocate for young German Jews to immigrate to Palestine. He proclaimed this Zionist message in many lectures he gave all over Germany. But, crucially, he became aware that this was probably not a solution for older, less fit people, like himself.

His oldest son, Wolfgang Louis (known as Wölfl) went to France in 1933, forced to escape because at school he had been an active social democrat and thus anti-Nazi. His second son, Ernst Abraham, went to a kibbutz in Palestine in 1935, and, at the last minute, in 1940 his oldest daughter, Ruth, went to Palestine via a Zionist training camp in Denmark, and then Russia. In the latter part of the Second World War, a Jewish Legion was established within the British army, and both Wolfgang Louis and Ernst Abraham joined it.

In 1937, Willy and Gertrud visited Palestine, staying at Ernst's kibbutz and were soon considering emigration. But Gertrud was not impressed. She did not think that Palestine and kibbutz life suited her. On the other hand, Willy was enthused and highly emotional about visiting and travelling in *Eretz Israel* (Land of Israel). He made many enquiries and had many discussions about getting some kind of job there, presumably in his fields of teaching and research. But he came to realise that he was too old to move there, and lacking in fluency in Hebrew, he would not be able to make a living as a teacher or researcher. When they returned to Breslau, there still seemed to be some possibility of a move to Palestine. Later, when the war started and the situation in Breslau worsened, they applied again to move to Palestine (in spite of Gertrud's doubts), but "certificates" for immigration to Palestine (determined by the British administration of the Palestine mandate) had become very scarce and they did not get support from the kibbutz.

At that point, or even earlier, Gertrud had felt that they should move to the USA. But Willy was not willing. He wanted to emigrate to Palestine and nowhere else. This led to regular unpleasant discussions between them. Would a move to the USA have been practicable? It was the most popular destination for German Jewish refugees. But such visas for the USA became more and more scarce. Gertrud made many attempts to get the necessary visas but was not successful. Yet there were other possibilities. In 1941, Gertrud's elderly parents living in Berlin moved to Argentina, and then, later moved on to the USA. Willy's uncle, Moritz (brother of his father) and before him his children, had also moved to Argentina.

It seems to me that there were possibilities—even Australia—and Gertrud's well-off parents could have financed a move for their daughter and her family. Here I am speculating. On the basis of some remarks he made in his autobiography, I suspect that (given that he did not get on with his mother-in-law) Willy was too proud to ask for help and would not have accepted if it had been offered. That was just his way.

It seems that Willy did not want to move to anywhere other than Palestine and indeed had doubts about Palestine for the reasons given above. Why was he so reluctant to move?

He gave four reasons at different times or places. First, he was too old and unwell to move (owing to a heart condition), lacking in energy, and really just wanted to die in Breslau. Comparing him with my father, it is relevant that Willy was eight years older. Second, he would not be able to adapt to a new location, or adapt sufficiently to make a living, and did not want to become a "beggar" (that pride again), and thirdly he loved Germany too much, which may have meant that he loved his existing work, social circle and physical environment, and also his books, and fourthly that he had a duty to the Breslau Jewish community to stay till the end. One might describe this latter explanation as a case of the captain not leaving a sinking ship (my term). He was certainly a committed and highly involved member of the Breslau Jewish community, who was devoted up to the end in tidying up its records.

With regard to loving Germany, he had a lifelong commitment to the German language owing to his massive amount of writing. Also, he had been teaching German literature. In fact, in spite of "assimilation" issues to be discussed below, he was actually highly assimilated not to the Germany of Hitler or even the Kaiser (for whom he had fought in the war) but to the Germany of Goethe, Schiller, and Heine. Can one blame him? I shall come back to his interesting attitude to Germany and the international policies of the Nazis.

In my view, with financial help from his in-laws, he and his immediate family of four might have been able to emigrate to somewhere, even perhaps the USA. He was fortunate to have a much younger, healthier, and capable wife. I could imagine her organising everything, and in their new location, she would go to work while he stayed at home attending to the children and spent his time working on his historical research and publishing in German. There may also have been light part-time jobs for him, as many immigrants of his age have found. But an obstacle was his pride. I wish he had left the crucial decision to his wife.

All this is speculation on my part, based on limited information, and may seem unfair or even cruel, given what happened. He was an outstanding and creative personality faced with a tragic situation. Perhaps, given his mental and physical condition, it was not a tragedy that he died the terrible way he did, but certainly it was a tragedy for Gertrud and the two little girls.

Why Did Willy and Rudolf Follow Different Paths?

To Willy, Judaism was central to his life. He was heavily committed to the Breslau Jewish community and judged every event or situation by how it affected Jews. He disapproved of Jews who became secular (not practising) or even worse, actually converted to a Christian denomination (usually Lutheran). He strongly disapproved of intermarriage with a non-Jew (as in my case), and he disapproved when Jews changed a name from a Jewish to a non-Jewish name (as my family did in Australia). In fact, many German Jews—including many of his relatives—committed some of these "sins". Before the Nazi period, many German Jews (like my father) also opposed Zionism because they feared that if they supported Zionism, Germans would then accuse them of having a dual loyalty, and they desperately wanted to be accepted as "real Germans". Actually, Willy was also a German patriot, partly as a result of his war service, but he felt he could reconcile this with his Jewishness and Zionism.

It is interesting to contrast my father, Rudolf, with Willy. My father never wrote down his thoughts, but I have a clear picture of his views. He simply regarded being labelled as a Jew by one's birth as a big disability. Unlike Willy, he had no pride in being Jewish. This was reasonable given the situation in Germany—with widespread anti-Semitism even before the Nazi takeover—and, as I have noted in Chap. 2, in fact going back to the nineteenth century. One needs to remember Heine, whose views he shared. No doubt it would not be reasonable today in many countries, like the USA or Australia.

A careful reading of the first chapter of Willy's autobiography gives me an explanation of why the two brothers formed radically different views about the role of Judaism in their lives.

When their father, Louis, died unexpectedly at the age of 60, Willy was 15. His father was a fairly observant Jew, not orthodox but a regular attendant at the Breslau Reform Synagogue (the New Synagogue). Every Friday evening, Willy would pick him up at Trautner, and they would go together to the synagogue. Willy was devoted to, and much influenced by, his father. And Louis ensured they had a Jewish home, following the main customs. His own father had actually been a rabbi. By contrast,

Rudolf was only seven when their father died, and thus he was probably much more influenced by his mother, Margaret, born a Hainauer. While Louis could trace his ancestry to Provinz Posen, the Hainauers—a prominent family of music publishers—had been several generations in Germany and were much influenced by the Enlightenment. They were highly sceptical about religion. Indeed, to Willy's horror, their uncle, brother of their mother, was almost cynical about Jewish customs and manners. Incidentally, it seems that Willy was influenced by his mother in one respect—she especially encouraged his intellectual and academic interests, which thus resulted in his choice of career.

Who Was Right and Who Was Wrong?

It is sad that Willy and Rudolf had a feud on an important issue, to the point where they hardly talked to each other. They were both intolerant.

It is interesting to reflect many years later who was right and who was wrong. Willy decided after the First World War that there was no future for Jews in Germany because Jews were blamed for Germany losing the war, even though many fought, died, or were injured fighting for Germany. He himself had received the Iron Cross. As I have already mentioned, as a result he became a keen Zionist, and two of his older children eventually settled in Palestine. He gave lectures urging young Jews to immigrate to Palestine. By contrast, Rudolf was an "assimilationist". He had little belief in the Jewish religion and (like a majority of German Jews) just thought Jews should assimilate. It is obvious that Willy was right.

But in another respect, Rudolf was right. Willy did not approve of Breslau Jews going to the USA (or the UK or Australia). It was "deserting the community". The only place to go to was Palestine. Implicitly he believed that assimilating in any of those countries was "deserting the community" (just like assimilating to the Germans) and, in any case, would not succeed. And here, Rudolf was right. In those countries assimilation has worked, both for those Jews who (more or less) abandoned their religion (like me) and those who kept it. What did not succeed in Germany did succeed in the USA, UK, Australia, Canada, certainly France and probably Argentina, and some other countries.

Incidentally, Willy was an active social democrat. He had high moral standards. I suspect if he had settled in Israel he would have been a "peace now" supporter and disapproved of the treatment of the Arabs, and of the militant right-wing parties. He would have been disappointed by the policies of Israeli governments since 1967.

Willy's Surprising Attitude to Germany

Willy's attitude to Germany is surely surprising, at least seen with hindsight. The DVD of a film about Willy produced for Rundfunk Berlin-Brandenburg is entitled (I translate) *The Jew who loved Germany: The Diaries of Willy Cohn.* In his diaries, he makes various remarks that indicated sympathy for German international grievances. Here is a quotation from the English translation of the Breslau Diaries. He is commenting on a Hitler speech in January 1939. "I can understand that the German people needs living space, and if that living space had been granted, this enmity towards the Jews in Germany would never have developed."

There are also other remarks of this kind. One wonders how much of this is explained by patriotic feelings developed during his war service and how much reflected his many years of teaching German history and literature at the Johannes Gymnasium. Of course, one can understand criticism of the harshness of the Versailles Treaty, put most clearly in a famous book by John Maynard Keynes, but this does not justify, for example, the invasions of Austria and Czechoslovakia. One might conclude that, in spite of his commitment to Judaism and later Zionism, Willy was indeed highly assimilated to Germany, like so many other German Jews. From his point of view, the tragedy was that this devotion was not accepted by the German people.

Why My Parent's Prediction About Me Was Only Partly True

Finally, I come back to the issue raised at the beginning of this chapter. Did I take after Uncle Willy?

I became an academic, which Willy would have become if his Jewishness had not been an obstacle. Before 1933, he could have obtained a university post if he had been prepared to convert and give up Judaism. But he was a proud Jew. I published many articles and books, though far fewer than he had. I became a committed teacher, as did Willy. I was inclined to put my thoughts down on paper, as certainly was Willy. Indeed, we have both written our autobiographies! And I spent a life devoted to books, as did Willy. But there was one big difference. I have not been a practising Jew. In this respect I followed my father, of whom Uncle Willy strongly disapproved.

As an afterthought, let me add another similarity which follows from our "bookishness". Willy was deeply attached to German culture, and especially literature, in spite of all that was happening in Germany. I was attached to British culture, and especially literature, in spite of growing up far away from Britain. It is also relevant that Willy was a historian and that I might have become a historian if my father had not directed me into economics via commerce.

Willy Always Remembered

Speech of the Bundespräsident

On 27 January 2015 (Day of Remembrance of the Victims of National Socialism), the Bundespräsident of Germany made a moving speech that referred at length to Willy. (The speech was on the web in English translation.) He quoted from Willy's diary, making the point what a loss it was to Germany by losing Willy and others. This is what Willy wrote in his diary: "I love Germany so much that this love cannot be shaken, not even by all these troubles. … One has to be loyal enough to submit to a government that comes from a completely different political camp." I think this would have been written by Willy during the early stages of the Nazi takeover.

Life Under Nazi Rule

In Tamar Gazit's *Life Under Nazi Rule*, there is a concise account of life under Nazi rule for the Jewish community of Breslau during 1933–1941, drawing on various documents and especially Willy's diaries. The author is an Israeli granddaughter of Willy. This is available on the web.

A Film About Willy

As mentioned above, there is a DVD of a film about Willy entitled *Ein Jude der Deutschland liebte* (A Jew who loved Germany). It was filmed first in Breslau and then in Israel (in the kibbutz where Ernst was), and finally in the Catholic Cathedral. A voice cites extracts from the diaries. This is a very moving film directed by Dr Petra Lidschreiber and sponsored and shown in 2008 on Rundfunk Berlin-Brandenburg. A version with English subtitles is available.

How the Diaries and the Autobiography Survived

The diaries covered the whole period from (about) 1909 to 1941. When, in 1941, Willy was informed that he and his family would have to vacate their apartment and be sent away, he arranged for the diaries to be deposited with Mr and Mrs Zeitz in Berlin. Mrs Zeitz was a cousin of his first wife, and hence Jewish, while Mr Zeitz was non-Jewish ("Aryan") and a railway official. Willy realised that the diaries would be safer if held by an "Aryan". In addition, there were the memoirs, dictated at the last stage in 1940 and 1941. This was the autobiography, which covered his life up to 1933. Here also one copy was deposited with the Zeitz couple, but there was a second copy deposited at the Cathedral Archives.

The son of the Zeitz couple, Wolfgang Zeitz, went to England before the war. After a period of internment, by the end of the war, he was in the British army. In 1945, when Berlin lay in ruins, he went with an "Advance Detachment" of the British Army to the British Zone, acting as interpreter. He found his parents. They had been bombed out and lived in a cellar.

They had taken Willy's manuscripts with them to the cellar. Wolfgang contacted the Proskauer family in New York and they, in turn, contacted Willy's two sons, both in the Jewish Legion of the British army. They could not actually go to Berlin but arranged for all the manuscripts (diaries and memoirs) to be sent from Berlin to London, where there was another relative. Later, in 1960, Ernst Abraham went to London to study and then brought these precious documents back with him to Israel. He then translated them into Hebrew, a massive enterprise. Finally, they were deposited in the Central Archive for History of the Jewish People in Jerusalem.

The final, very important, part of the story is that Professor Norbert Conrads of Stuttgart University, a specialist on Silesian history (and born in Breslau) heard about the memoirs and the diaries and undertook the massive task of editing them for German publication. To be precise, the memoirs or autobiography (Verwehte Spuren 1995) cover the whole of Willy's life up to 1933, while the published diaries (Kein Recht, Nirgends 2006) only cover, but in great detail, the Nazi period from 1933 to 1941. It is the latter that has made the biggest impact.

In addition, a condensed version in English of the diaries of 1933–1941 is available. This has also been edited by Norbert Conrads but translated by Kenneth Kronenberg. Furthermore, there is a Hebrew edition of these diaries, translated by his son Ernst Abraham (as noted above) and edited by Tamar Gazit, and published in 2014 by The Hebrew University Magnes Press, Jerusalem.

The Family Lives, Especially as Teachers

I obtained the following information with the help of Tamar Gazit, granddaughter of Willy.

Three of Willy's children survived the Holocaust, namely Wolfgang Louis (Wolfl) and Ernst Abraham from the first marriage and Ruth from the second. Wolfl had lived in France and Ernst and Ruth in Israel. By 2016, all three had passed away. Now, let me list the next generation. It consists of two daughters of Wolfl, Danielle and Francoise; three children of Ernst, Tamar, Nurit, and Amos; and two daughters of Ruth, Talma and Orit.

Now, how many of this generation became teachers and thus followed in the footsteps of Willy? Answer: *five*, namely Danielle, Francoise, Tamar, Amos, and Talma. And one should really add Wolfl, who was a teacher in France. Furthermore, one might add two of Willi's nephews, Max (me) and Paul (son of Willy's sister Erna Proskauer, who immigrated to New York), and we get *eight*.

Surely, there is a family tradition!

Bibliography

Cohn, Willy *Autobiography, Verwehte Spuren*, published by Norbert Conrads, 1995.

Cohn, Willy, *No Justice in Germany, Kein Recht Nirgends*, published by Norbert Conrads 1933–41.

Cohn, Willy, *No Justice in Germany: The Breslau Diaries 1933–41*. Condensed English edition, published by Norbert Conrads and translated by Kenneth Kronenberg 2012.

4

The Promised Land: Migrating to the Lucky Country

The Journey

The four of us—father, mother, Gerhart, and I—left Southampton for Australia on 16 December 1938; indeed, a historic day. The Dutch liner, the *Sibajak*, belonged to Rotterdamsche Lloyd and had come to Southampton from Rotterdam. Aunt Elli had brought Gerhart and me to the port and waved us goodbye.

There were 144 other German Jews on the boat. A few couples came from Breslau, including Mr. and Mrs. Hecht and their daughter. We have a photo showing me, Werner (aged 11), teaching English to Mr. Hecht. Gerhart and I spoke English with each other. I ate in a separate dining room with other small children, while Gerhart (aged 16) ate with the adults. After Lisbon, Tangier, Marseilles (freezing), Port Said, and Aden, we reached Colombo, where we got out. We stayed one night at the Grand Oriental Hotel and then boarded the *Oronsay* belonging to the British Orient Line, to take us to Australia.

Who paid for this journey? We (the family) did. In Germany, we were not allowed to take out any money at all, nor things that could be converted into money, notably jewellery. But we could use our own German money to pay for transport. Anything that was left presumably just went

© The Author(s) 2017   **41**
W.M. Corden, *Lucky Boy in the Lucky Country*, Palgrave Studies in the History of
Economic Thought, DOI 10.1007/978-3-319-65166-8_4

to the German government. So my parents bought four tickets to Sydney, which we had chosen as our destination.

Who Should We Thank?

To get to Australia, we needed visas, the most precious documents, which, in fact, saved our lives. Who should we thank for these? Apparently, after Kristallnacht and after much discussion, the Australian government decided to accept 15,000 German and Austrian Jews over three years, at the rate of 5000 per year. The key persons to thank for this generous decision were John McEwen, the Minister for the Interior in the Lyons government, and Stanley Bruce, the Australian High Commissioner in London (Blakeney, *Australia and the Jewish Refugees*). The decision was supported by John Curtin, the Leader of the (Labor) Opposition, and also by the *Sydney Morning Herald* newspaper, and by (Catholic) Archbishop Mannix.

Only 5000 came under the programme because of the outbreak of war in September 1939. We were just four of these 5000.

The further question is: How did we get to be the lucky four? In this respect, I do not know the details. The selection would probably have been made at Australia House in London, and I guess or assume that our wonderful Aunt Elli played a crucial role. I also note that in February 1938, my father went from Breslau to London for a month and possibly played a role in the process.

The Adelaide Shock

Our first stop was Fremantle. All I remember is that I was photographed in front of the tall War Memorial on a hill inland somewhere. Then the ship went on to Adelaide through the Great Australian Bight, which was rough.

But Adelaide was a shock. We stayed there for less than a day. It was January 1939. It was incredibly hot (100 degrees?). What a country had we come to! Father had some people or persons to contact and went off to "do business", whatever that was. The three of us walked around. I remember nothing except for the extreme heat. I can only imagine what my parents were thinking. Presumably after Buchenwald (which Gerhart and I knew nothing about) anything else was better, but this. So, back on the *Oronsay* by 1.00 p.m. and two days later, at night we saw the lights of Melbourne as we steamed through Port Philip Bay. After the ship berthed, we were informed that we must stay in the cabins until the next morning, when police would inspect our "papers".

With regard to the Adelaide heat, a memoir that Gerhart has written and I read only recently (January 2017), says that our mother feared "she had come from one hell to another!"

Melbourne! Fantastic Weather

When we stepped off the ship in Melbourne, it was 25 January 1939, a memorable day in our lives. While we first touched Australian soil on 17 January (in Fremantle), it is the 25th, one day before Australia Day (the 26th) that is the really historic day, of which I can remember every hour. And the most memorable moment was when we left the cabin and went on deck—and discovered the climate!

Blue Sky and a Cool Breeze Unbelievable, after Adelaide. Perhaps we thought that Melbourne has such a wonderful climate and Adelaide such an awful one, but what I now understand is that South Australia (capital, Adelaide) and Victoria (capital, Melbourne) tend to have similar climates, and January is the period of heat waves and bushfires—as it was then— and the changes from extreme heat (with winds from the north) to comfortable mild weather (the winds coming from the west) can be very sudden. Indeed, the change in this case took place while we were on the high seas travelling from Adelaide to Melbourne. The westerly winds are more normal and give southern Australia a delightful Mediterranean climate.

It took about two hours to get our "papers" checked and bring up our luggage. And then Mrs. Coyne of the Jewish Welfare Committee drove us down St. Kilda Road to a boarding house in Westbury Street, St. Kilda. Driving down St. Kilda Road, a boulevard (with trams travelling down the middle) reminded me of Kaiser Wilhelm Strasse in Breslau. My father was tremendously impressed and relieved, and both Gerhart and I remember him saying (in German, of course) "this is the most beautiful street in the world". The total effect was that, after a long journey, stopping at many non-European cities (notably Port Said, Aden, Colombo), here we were in a highly European city and country. Perhaps he was exaggerating a little, but even now St. Kilda Road is a fine street, though modern architecture has not always improved it. But on one side there is a fine long stretch of parkland.

In a few days, the ship was due to sail off to Sydney, which was our destination. But in Melbourne, my father must have met some local Jewish people, who persuaded him that Melbourne might be more suitable. I guess that would have been because the Jewish community in Melbourne was significantly bigger than the one in Sydney. Therefore, we settled in Melbourne. A crate of furniture (and some books) had been sent from Breslau to Sydney, which my parents arranged to be redirected later.

Our First Home

After a few weeks in the boarding house, we rented our first home in Melbourne. This was a small single storey, two-bedroom house in Evelyn Street, St Kilda. Naturally, Gerhart and I shared a room, and he drew (with a string) a line down the middle to make clear how far I might go. The street ran off a main street, Inkerman Road, and was a short dead-end street so that there was almost zero traffic. But my first memory is of great excitement. One could open the kitchen door and could then walk into the back garden, which was indeed small (with the usual Hills-hoist for hanging laundry). And from there, one could walk out into the street. But, having lived in Breslau on the fifth floor (without a lift) of a large apartment building, where every venture out of doors required indeed a boring journey down many stairs, it was exciting to be able to step out, just like that. Indeed, I kept on going in and out, banging the kitchen door. Eventually, I had to be stopped. This was my first tremendously favourable experience in Australia. Another thing I remember is that in the evening until quite late, say 8.00 or 9.00 p.m., children, some of my age, would play in front of our house, while I was expected to go to bed. This was a little indication of the contrasting culture into which we were moving.

A big issue that I have not firmly resolved is how our rent and indeed living costs were financed in those early days. It took a while for my father to generate an income, and the Germans stopped us from leaving with any money at all. There seem to be two explanations. I believe that my parents borrowed some money from friends from Germany (the Aarons), who had left Breslau a year earlier than us but gone to the USA. I think they changed their name to Anrode. Dr Anrode was a doctor and, I think, practised in Davenport, Iowa. I think that my parents repaid this debt but have no written evidence of all this. In addition, it is highly likely that we received a grant or loan from the Victorian Jewish Welfare Society.

Change of Names

Very soon we arranged for a change of names. Many of the German Jewish immigrants anglicised their names in various ways, and we did also. Uncle Willy would not have approved. There have been many derivations of the historic Jewish name of Cohn or Cohen, and we picked another one that was a known but not very popular British name, namely Corden. Some Australian acquaintance of my father suggested it.

Since then I have discovered that there are quite a few Cordens in the world, including one who was in the (Australian) First Fleet, and a recent well-known British actor, James Corden (with a son named Max). The dictionary of English surnames reports that this name may have originated from Spanish leather made originally at Cordoba. I have also heard that it may have a Cornish origin.

The main problem with the name was that my father had difficulty in pronouncing the letter R in an English or Australian way. If he was asked to spell his name, the R would come out as a hard German RRR. The name Gerhart became, obviously Gerald, but my own change was not so obvious. Werner became Warner, and the derivation of the latter may be from the German, with many British people having Warner as a surname. But mine was a first name. At that time, there was a minor Hollywood actor named Warner Baxter, so it seemed an OK choice. But Warner as a first name was not, in my view, a good choice, so at some stage I decided to make use of my middle name, Max, which I kept from Melbourne High School on. I am still Warner Max on my passport and various other documents, but my first books (1971–1977) simply had W M and later I switched to W Max and got everyone to call me Max. My parents at home always used the German names, while their sons socially and at school commonly became Gerry and Max.

Here I must add something else which is surprising. The gentleman who advised my father to choose the name Corden in the belief that it was a way of making our name less Jewish and more British must have been guided by a Holy Hand—or perhaps the Spirit of Uncle Willy.

One of the greatest Jews that ever lived was Moses ben Maimon, better known as Maimonides, the famous scholar-philosopher, who lived and worked in Cairo, Egypt. He was born in Cordoba, Spain in 1135! He was best known for his book *Guide of the Perplexed*. He also wrote *Treatise on Logic*, and he was a practising medical doctor. In Johnson's *A History of the Jews*, where I got this information, he is described as "a rationalist by temperament" and that, "above all, he was a scientist, looking for truth, confident it would prevail at the end". May I say that, in hindsight, he has been my role model, especially in writing economics. It is an honour to have by accident (almost) the name of his city of birth as my surname.

My Father's and Mother's Businesses

Name change is a trivial matter. More important was the need for my father to build up a business of some kind so as to earn an income. He set out to become a manufacturers' agent and wholesaler, primarily for ladies' handbags (and possibly other fashion goods). For that, he set out to build relationships with German and Austrian immigrants, who did the manufacturing. Also, he would import some of the goods. He wanted to become Victorian agent (and possibly also for Adelaide) for these goods. Some of his suppliers lived and worked in Melbourne, but, I think, more of them were in Sydney. Once he got this going, he seemed to do quite well. In those days, Australia had import controls, which were frequently changed by the government, and I used to hear much about this at the dinner table. Changes could have big effects on his business. This stimulated my interest in these controls, which I wrote about later, when I became an economist.

His real ability was in selling. His customers were ladies, who did the buying for stores, both large department stores and small shops. It clearly helped that he got on well with women and was very likeable. His most important customers were in the big cities, Melbourne and Adelaide. But he also travelled regularly to smaller country towns in Victoria. He would stay at the principal (or only) hotel, join the local males in the bar, and the next day visit his customers, who would welcome him warmly.

I would generalise that he was a natural salesman but not necessarily a natural businessman. He was a "people person". He had a base or office in a room in Little Collins Street in downtown Melbourne. In later years (after the war), my mother joined him. She did the office side rather than selling. At various stages, he employed other people, especially a devoted Australian secretary and a more junior Australian salesman.

I attach here a letter which is my translation into English of a letter in German he wrote six months after arriving in Australia to his mother, his sister Erna, and his brother Willy, all still in Breslau. It is the only letter of his that I have. Thus, I have nothing else in writing about his views. He was indeed very different from Willy. The letter was kept by Erna's family, who eventually went to New York, and it was sent to me many years later by Norbert Conrads when Erna's son (Paul) had died, and it was found among his papers. It tells us that my father was finding it extremely hard to build up his business, but his impression of Australians and Australia (and especially of Sydney) was very favourable.

Once Japan got into the war, the Australian government established a "Pioneer Corps" for immigrants to get into the army and do non-combatant work. This has been much written about. Now in his 40s, he became a corporal and wore an Australian military uniform. Of course, he had also been a corporal in the Kaiser's army in the First

World War. This meant that his family now received an income similar to what other Australian dependants of the military received. This was not vast but eased the financial pressure on our family. After the war, he went back to the business, which had been kept going during the war by an employee.

He died unexpectedly of a heart attack in 1958 at the age of 62. He was doing business in Adelaide, where he went regularly every year.

For a little while, after he died, the business continued in a reduced size with my mother managing it and one salesman-employee. Gerald and I did an analysis of the business and found that his agent work was profitable but his wholesale business was not. Thus, it was possible to reduce the scope of the business and actually increase profits somewhat.

Naturalisation 1944

A little over five years after arrival (January 1939) we were all naturalised—all in 1944, but oddly, not on the same day. So we became Australian citizens. At that time, my father was in the Army.

Gerald	6 March
Ralph (Rudolf) and Max	29 May
Katherine (Kate)	11 August

Source: ICSE Index (Dept. of Immigration)

Back to the Early Days

Now, let me get back to the early days after we arrived in Australia.

My mother built up a small business of her own, which kept going during the period when my father was in the army. This was also based in Melbourne, in an office in Collins Street. She had a machine with which she could make covered belts and buckles for dressmakers. The dressmakers would supply the material, my mother would use that for covering belts and buckles, and then the finished product would be returned to the dressmaker. For some time, I would work there after school, picking up the material and delivering the covered belts and buckles. The important thing was to do it all correctly and not mix up the dressmakers. The latter worked in offices in Melbourne, especially the big Manchester Unity Building, and I would be going up and down lifts. It was a good experience for learning to be polite and efficient.

Gerald, aged 16, studied at the Royal Melbourne Institute of Technology (RMIT and now RMIT University). He obtained diplomas in mechanical and electrical engineering, but the mechanical engineering diploma was the relevant one for his subsequent work. He has worked as an engineer for two major companies, namely first Monsanto and then for 30 years, from 1947, for Rocla. This was when his mechanical engineering work really started.

The main work of this company was the manufacture of concrete pipes. The company had developed a novel method of making concrete pipes, and this was sold all over the world. It actually became a kind of multinational company. They built factories in Britain and Canada and exported machinery and technology to many other countries including France, Germany, and Mexico. Gerald visited many countries and enjoyed travel. He was on his way to Germany when we crossed paths in Paris in 1955, and Dorothy (my future wife) arrived from Melbourne. After he retired from the company in 1977, he continued with consulting in the field, working from home.

I, Max, went to four different state schools, one after the other. I will describe my experiences at all these schools in Chap. 5.

The last school was Melbourne High School (MHS), where I went from 1942 to 1945, turning 18 in 1945. That year ended my early seven-year period in Australia, which was for me, my adolescent period. Above all, it included the war period, 1940–1945. After that I went to University from 1946 to 1949, then had two jobs (first *The Argus* newspaper, and then a Commonwealth government department based in Melbourne) and then off to England to begin my career as an economist. From 1947 to 1949, I was a resident at Queen's College (attached to Melbourne University), where I made some very good friends.

My First Period in Australia: Impressions

Thinking back on comparisons with Germany, what were my impressions of Australians, and those of my parents', during that early seven-year period?

I had two main impressions, the first the dominant one.

Firstly, Australians were very friendly. I found this everywhere, especially with teachers and also fellow students at schools. And my parents had the same impression, notably with neighbours. What a contrast with Germany! This also meant that we did not suffer from anti-Semitic hostility. On that subject, I was paranoid. Perhaps bad things may have been said about me behind my back, but I doubt it. There was just one minor anti-Semitic episode at MHS in 1945, but that was the only one in four years.

My parents also noticed this friendliness. They had a lot of contact with Australians through their contacts with neighbours and their work and got on extremely well with many people. One lady, Mrs. Marsland, who worked as secretary for my father, was absolutely devoted to him. And he got on well with all the ladies to whom he sold or tried to sell handbags. It is also my impression (though I did not observe it) that he got on well with Australian men both in the army and in hotels (pubs) in country towns. It helped that he was exceptionally outgoing.

Coming back to my schools, it helped that I did not stick with fellow immigrants but made a point of becoming friendly with Australian boys. I think Australians don't like it when immigrants form groups, and I made sure that I never got into that position. At Melbourne High School, there were five German Jews (including myself) in my year, and I deliberately stayed away from the other four, staying in a class where I was the only one. In addition, I was deliberately reticent and tried to stay in the background.

My mother, who was quite elegant (and sometimes was thought to be French), was liked and respected, though she had no close Australian friends. Of course, she got on well with all the dressmakers. My parents' close friends were all fellow German Jews, some from Breslau. I don't think there were any close Australian friends.

But there was a second observation (or confession) I should make, and this only concerned myself, neither my parents nor my brother.

I was aware that there was in Australia a lot of hostility towards us, that is towards Jews or "reffos" (short for refugees). To some extent this was just old-fashioned anti-Semitism. Amazingly (with one exception), I never ever met anyone who was hostile, but this hostility existed in print. I (secretly) bought several newspapers or magazines which regularly had hostile articles, notably *The Bulletin* and *Smiths Weekly*, and also *Truth*. I used to buy *Smiths Weekly* regularly at the newspaper shop at the South Yarra Railway Station but never let my parents see it. There were also letters to the editor in *The Argus*. The RSL (Returned Servicemen's League) was clearly hostile. All this had a macabre fascination for me. It was not healthy that I had this obsession. And, in spite of this, my academic career at MHS flourished.

Coming back to my parents, in the early days at least, their main preoccupation was to get established and focus on survival. Unlike me, they had no time for obsessions. Furthermore, my father was so relieved that he was in a country that treated him reasonably, and where we were all safe. I think to treat him and others as "enemy aliens" when the war began was humiliating and unnecessary (we actually were not German nationals when we arrived but were stateless), but I don't think he minded it. Everything was better than Germany! Incidentally, the term "enemy alien" was copied from Britain.

Let me end with one memorable recollection. At the end of my schooling at MHS, I won a Senior Scholarship—not from the school but from the State of Victoria on the basis of the state examination—to go to university. This meant that there would be no fees, and that I had got high marks. My father was impressed, not that I had done well but that—in spite of being an immigrant (and a Jew!)—I had been awarded a scholarship by the government. This could not have happened in Germany!

Appendix

This is my translation of a letter which my father wrote (in German) in 1939 to his mother, his brother (Willy), and his sister (Erna Proskauer) in Breslau. It is the only letter of his which I have, and thus is a great family heirloom. Later, the Proskauers went to America and lived in New York. The letter was kept by them, and when their younger son Paul died at the age of 90, it was found by whoever went through his papers. It was sent to me by Norbert Conrads (in 2013). This letter was written five months after we arrived in Melbourne. My grandmother (Grossmutti Cohn, mother of my father) was unwell and died peacefully in September 1939. Willy, Trudi, and their two little girls were "transported" (murdered) in November 1941. I have included below some explanations in parentheses.

My Father's Letter to the Breslau Family 30 June 1939

I have a bad conscience that I have not written for such a long time. It is to be excused by our hard work (long hours). I work every night until 11.00 p.m. and the day begins at 6.45 a.m., without pause. You cannot conceive how hard it is to make a living here (earn money). But it goes forward slowly; we are making progress.

The previous week I was for one week on business in Sydney as I could use my unused ticket from Melbourne to Sydney.

Melbourne is indeed a nice city, but Sydney is a town that, in the beauty of its landscape is incomparable, surpasses any European city. Numerous small bays, with delightful houses, rise from hills out of the deep-blue sea. From every spot, there is a fabulous view. The whole town breathes the sunny nature, as also the inhabitants, who have or follow the Australian lifestyle of "take it easy".

I could tell you for hours about this journey. I travelled by steamer on the way to Sydney, the same ship that the Duke of Kent will travel in next October. I have eaten well (on the ship) at the expense of the ticket we had bought in Germany. On the return trip, I travelled by the pride of the Australian railway system, the Spirit of Progress, a magnificent streamliner.

Yes, you may think that here one sees kangaroos and wild animals, but it is not so. Also, so far, we have not seen a single aboriginal (the original inhabitants).

As I have mentioned, we have to work very hard for all these attractions, and I cannot say that we are yet over the hill. I have received some new agencies, though this means more work. But I cannot afford to forego such opportunities and must take what is available.

(He was trying to build up a business as a manufacturer's agent, that is as commercial traveller, and some (or all?) of them were manufacturers based in Sydney. I think women's handbags (and ladies' accessories) was the main product.)

Katel (my mother Kate) is busy with her collars and buttons as we wish to launch a new collection soon.

Gerhart has just done his first exam. We don't yet know the result, but I am not worried. The boys are really a great support; they help in everything. Enough about us.

I am very sad that you, dear Mother, suffer from pains. I hope they will pass soon. For your good wishes, just received, I thank you 1000 times. On this day (her birthday?) I shall think of you with longing, and many memories of better days and worry-free times come to me. But what does it help? One has to look to the future.

Dear Willy and dear Trudi, thank you for your informative letter that shows me that you have not forgotten your Latin (he then quotes a Latin sentence). I hope that your plans will develop and come true. I don't think that your idea to write for Jewish newspapers is likely to be successful. But write me two letters to Australian newspapers (to the *Australian Jewish Herald* and the *Australian Jewish News*), which I will forward.

The letters from you, dear Proskauers, have made me very sad. I have not forgotten you. In Sydney, I exchanged recollections (memories) with the Sterns. But I don't agree that we will never meet again. Once you are in America, it is not so far. Raise your head high, it will be OK. I have written an urgent letter to Julia to help you with entry to England. (They were worried about their future. He is trying to help them get entry to England, I think. Actually, it worked out alright; they settled eventually in New York.)

Now I am so tired my eyes are closing, I can't keep awake.

(All this is typed. He ends in handwriting, with love and so on. Also, there are hand-written illegible greetings from my mother at the end. She writes in German script, of the kind that I learnt at school).

Bibliography

Blakeney, Michael, *Australia and the Jewish Refugees 1933–48*, 1984
Johnson, Paul *A History of the Jews,* 1987.

5

My Seven Schools

I begin with Breslau. My first school was the *Gaudigschule* (near the *Süd-Park*). This was a state school, which according to the government all Jewish children had to leave at the end of 1935 (when I was eight and a half years old). I really liked Herr Blumel, my class teacher, and can still visualise him. That is all I remember.

The school reports show that I was good (*Gut*) in most subjects, including behaviour except in one quarter only, and very good in reading. But I was no good in music either failing (*Mangelhaft*) or *Unmusikalisch* and only adequate (*Genügent*) in gymnastics (*Turnen*).

I have indeed never managed to play a musical instrument, not even the piano, while at the same time I have a love of classical music. I do not think of myself as *Unmusikalisch*.

From 1936 to the first quarter of 1938, I went to the small Jewish school called the *Wohlschule* run by Gertrude Wohl. My teacher was either Miss Wohl or Fraulein Karfunkelstein. I did not like Fraulein K., and I can also still visualise her.

At both schools, my closest friend was Ulrich Batzdorf, the son of a doctor. He and his family immigrated to the USA in 1939, and, like me, he also went to an English boarding school first. We maintained contact for many years.

© The Author(s) 2017
W.M. Corden, *Lucky Boy in the Lucky Country*, Palgrave Studies in the History of
Economic Thought, DOI 10.1007/978-3-319-65166-8_5

Looking at my school reports from these school years, it is clear that I was basically average (*Gut*), except that my behaviour, attention, order, and so on were very good (*Sehr gut*), as sometimes was *Heimatskunde* (geography/history). But gymnastics was only adequate, while music was either adequate or *Mangelhaft*.

Here I must make an observation. This period at the Jewish *Wohlschule* clearly left me with the belief that, while very well behaved, I was just average—and certainly not one of the best. This has had an important effect on my judgement of myself. It made me modest.

I also have my certificate from the *Hallenschwimmbad* in Breslau (public indoor swimming pool) certifying that I fulfilled my 20-minute test on 9 June 1936. I remember that I was nervous and not a good swimmer compared to some other children. Like all German children at that time, I learnt breaststroke. In spite of moving to Australia at the age of 11, I never really learnt to swim the Australian crawl properly. But I am still fit, and indeed in recent years swim daily!

In May 1938, I began two terms at the Streete Court School in Westgate-on-Sea, near Margate, Kent, England. This was a private school that prepared children for English public (private) schools. I believe my stay there was financed by Woburn House (UK Jewish welfare) or specifically by a Lady Meyer. It was Anglican.

I have a long and fascinating letter about the school that Mr Hoare, the very kind headmaster, aged only 30, wrote to my father a week after I arrived. He gave a full account of the school's history and features and also about himself. He had travelled extensively on the Continent and taught since the age of 22. There were 35 students. I was put in a class of seven boys, who were generally a year younger than me. (I was aged 11 years and 4 months and the average age of the class was 10 years and 9 months.)

When I arrived, I knew no English and everything seemed a mystery to me. I can still recall some of the mysteries, above all cricket. When I was batting, why did the batsman opposite me not hit the ball back to me, as in tennis? There was also a problem that arose because I was not familiar with Christian customs. What did the three other boys in my room mean by "pray" when, before going to bed they wanted me to kneel at the bedside? Were they going to slap me on the behind? This puzzle came up on my very first night and was resolved when they brought in a German-speaking boy from another dormitory. Jews don't kneel; they bow.

After a little while, it was decided that some after-school extra tutoring in English was needed, and Mr. Browning got me to read from Shakespeare (yes!). Whenever I read about the poet Browning, I always have a visual picture of this Mr. Browning. On Sunday evenings, the headmaster would read stories to the boys, and at first it was all Greek to me, so I was absolutely bored.

At this school, I started studying French and Latin, both, of course, taught via English. Yet, my great strength was geography, and at the end of second term, I was first in the class in geography, being "Very Good". I knew, and everybody was told, that my family would be going to Australia, and this gave me a great sense of importance, when we had a lesson on Australia with a big map on the board, and I pointed out Sydney and perhaps other places. It is hard to believe, but according to the report, at the end of my second term, I came second (out of seven) in the class in Latin and French. Perhaps unsurprisingly in view of my later career (and the fact that I was older), I also came second in the three mathematics subjects (arithmetic, algebra, geometry). In his final report the headmaster wrote, "He has made more progress in Latin and French in two terms than many boys would make in two years". What I recall about the school was that everybody—teachers, my fellow students (only 35), and the headmaster's wife—were very kind.

When I came back to school from summer holidays in Dorset, I seemed to have found everything quite easy, and this must explain why I did so well. I have had nothing but fond memories of my experience at the school, and once in Australia, I kept thinking about it. Undoubtedly, it was at least a part-explanation for my later Anglophilism. At Melbourne High School, I was naturally drawn to an English-evacuee friend, and I loved English films.

It did not trouble me at all that one prayed every day, and that there was a regular Sunday church service that I always attended. In fact, I liked it. My parents had told me that I could always quietly say a Jewish prayer if I wanted to (I only knew one—the *shema yisrael*), which I did if I was worried about anything—for example when fielding at cricket in case the ball came my way. I prided myself on having learnt the Lord's Prayer and of course can still recite it.

My first school in Australia, in January 1939, was St. Kilda Park State School. I noticed the rubbish bins in the schoolyard, stuffed to overflowing with discarded lunches. Coming from Germany, where there was actually food rationing, and from Streete Court School and Westgate-on-Sea where everything was neat and clean, I was amazed at the waste of food.

A whole lot of immigrant Jewish children arrived at the same time and were lined up, apparently in order of size. I was very small so I was allocated to a class where I was two years older than other children. My parents were very worried about this and (as far as I can recall) they, with someone's help, must have complained and got me put up one class higher. As a result, I was still usually one of the oldest (or *the* oldest) in my class from then until I left Melbourne High at the age 18—though, being small, I did not look older.

Shortly afterwards (when we moved into our first home in St. Kilda), I was transferred to Brighton Road State School (next to the St. Kilda Town Hall). I was there for one year (1939). The class teacher used the strap (on the hand) and did so apparently every morning on some boys—though never on me. My main concern was survival by not being noticed and being always on my best behaviour. There were some pretty rough boys there, though they did me no harm. I don't recall any hostility. Rather there seemed to be a kind of war between the teacher and some of the boys, to which I was just an onlooker. Since I was such a goody-goody boy, the teacher probably viewed me with favour. On one occasion, one or more of the boys asked me whether I wanted to join them after school in "shop lifting in Carlisle Street". When I told my parents, they were absolutely aghast. Having just left a police state, and my father being let out of Buchenwald, the very idea horrified them.

I turned 13 in August 1940, and in preparation for my Bar Mitzvah at Temple Beth Israel, I went to Religious School. I have the report card. I was "Excellent" in history (which I greatly enjoyed) and surprisingly also in "Extra-curricular Activities", which refers to "an address and a project", which "have been an inspiration to the class" (I quote). But I was hopeless in Hebrew, getting a generous grade of "Fair". Nevertheless, while I was conscientious, I actually ceased to be a believer and stopped going to synagogue after the Bar Mitzvah except for some time on the twice-a-year special occasions (High Holidays). My very-Jewish analytical mind led me to analyse everything that was read and said at synagogue and converted me into a non-believer.

In 1940 and 1941, I went to Caulfield North Central School. That was another world from Brighton Road State. It was also a state school, and would lead subsequently to four years in a high school. It is located in Balaclava Road, near Caulfield Park. It still exists but under a different name. A pleasant and vivid memory is of newspaper-wrapped lunch bought sometimes at a fish-and-chip shop near the corner with the Park. (My mouth still waters at the thought.)

There were 39 in my class in 1940, and my form teacher was the lovely Miss Jones who, I believe, was just out of Teachers' College and aged 19. I was, as usual, shy and conscious of being small. Thus, it is amazing that I was appointed or elected form captain in the second term of 1940. This was the greatest honour I had ever achieved and, in terms of effect on me, it far outranks any honour I have received since. I was given the impression that I was elected, but it must have been arranged by the kind Miss Jones. I was very keen on drawing, especially architectural drawing of houses and streetscapes. This has been an obsession of mine and had begun already in Breslau. I remember my drawings being put up on the classroom wall. I came first in the class and got very high marks in every subject, with 100 for geography and for algebra and geometry. In every subject, I was far above the class average.

In 1941, the class number rose to 55, and the class averages for most subjects went up. I dropped to third in the class in one term and second in the other. But I received 100 for the three mathematics subjects each. I note this here. While an aptitude for mathematics is really essential for economics, I have always, by inclination, been a non-mathematical economist. I have always said that I could do my economics with more mathematics if I chose, but I don't choose to do it.

In 1942, I entered Melbourne High School (MHS). This is a selective state school. In fact, there were then only two such schools in Victoria, the other one being Mac.Robertson's Girls High School. MHS is now, as it was then, an outstanding school with about 1000 students, all boys.

Now an examination is required to enter the school, and students can come from any part of the state and any kind of school. At that time, in 1940, entry could only be from the general suburban area around the school and students were recommended by the central schools of the area.[1]

At some point, probably while I was at central school, or even in my first year at MHS, my parents had the thought that I might go to one of the (elite) private schools. Somebody must have told them that one gets the best education there and, through the contacts one makes while there, gets the best jobs. Of course, they could not really have afforded it. We were quite poor, and that was obvious to me. I absolutely refused not because I thought we could not afford it but because I would feel uncomfortable with fellow students from such well-off families. I knew that this was not our world. I have made bad decisions in life, but that was one of the best.

Caulfield North Central was in the area from where students could go to MHS. Hence it was not necessary for the Cordens to move away from St. Kilda for me to get in. But we did move from St. Kilda, namely to a location in the same street as MHS (Yarra Street, South Yarra), which probably was meant to make it easier for me to get to school. It was right next door to a yeast factory that spread a ghastly smell in our direction whenever the hot north wind blew. Our small apartment building, where we had a two-bedroom flat was still standing when I returned to Melbourne in 2002. I was told that it had for many years been a brothel.

Thus, I have a very fond memory of MHS. I found the teachers extremely sympathetic. I cannot recall that I disliked a single one, and some were inspiring—above all because of their commitment to their subjects.

As I look back, the biggest influences on me were not the teachers, nor the fellow students, but the books I read, especially in history and literature. Of course, I owe it to the school that it led one to read and study good books. And not everyone is as bookish as I was and am. By modern standards, the classes were large, but this did not trouble me at all. It was important that the general atmosphere among the staff and many of the students was academic. Sport and conversation about it were important—very important for some—but were not dominant the way it generally is in Australia.

MHS really was my world. I recall students who were interested in politics, especially the concern that the post-war should be better than the past. The past meant "the depression", which was a dominant memory for all parents, and two world wars. In those days, what happened in Britain was at least as important as what happened in Australia, and I recall the enthusiasm with which some (or many) students welcomed the unexpected and overwhelming victory of the British Labour Party in the 1945 elections. I shared this enthusiasm.

The headmaster in my first year, James Hill, was also an inspiration to me, and I have never forgotten him. He was already quite sick and died in 1943. His favourite song was "Jerusalem", which we all sang in chorus, and whenever I hear this wonderful, idealistic song, with the words by William Blake, I think of him. He has been described in the recent history of the school, "Strong Like its Pillars". I just felt that I was on his wavelength. I should add that at the first assembly in 1942 he (or was it one of the teachers?) gave a talk in which he told us that now that we are at MHS, we must really work. This is serious. And I took this seriously, possibly more than most students.

My own sole non-academic activity, apart from the minimum of sport (tennis), was to write some articles in *The Unicorn* (the school magazine). In 1944, I wrote about a cycling trip to Flinders, starting off with a quotation from Byron. Incidentally, long-distance cycling was actually my main sport, which I did with a somewhat eccentric fellow MHS student, Noel Stevens.

In my final year, graduating in 1945, there were five German Jewish boys, including myself. Three were in the science stream and went on to study medicine, the other two being Saul Dominitz and myself. *The Unicorn* of 1946 has photos of the 17 boys who won scholarships and exhibitions—that is, the academically most successful students of the year. Of these, four were German Jewish, including me.

At the final, state-wide examinations, I got first-class honours in four of my subjects, and a second-class honour in English literature. On the basis of these results, I received a General Exhibition (prize) as well as a senior scholarship to the university and a Queen's College scholarship. The switch to German from French was a bit of a cheat, and I should have stuck to French, though no doubt would not have managed a First. The French that I learnt up to Form V stood me in good stead in 1953, when I spent six weeks in France, hitchhiking, living on bread, tomatoes, and wine, staying in youth hostels (and at the end with my aunt Elli in Tourrettes-sur-Loup), and (other than at the end) speaking nothing but French.

Looking back, I have fondest memories of three schools—Streete Court in England, Caulfield Central, and Melbourne High. In all cases I felt at that time, and still remember, that the teachers were very good to me. I felt comfortable and appreciated. No doubt they had sympathy for me as a refugee. I suppose I rewarded them by being a well-behaved, goody-goody boy, never creating any trouble, and being a good student.

Notes

1. During the period that I wrote this memoir, a fine history of MHS was published—*Strong Like its Pillars* by Alan Gregory (who is a friend of mine and one of my former students from Melbourne University). I have aimed here not to be influenced by it here—other than getting some basic facts right—but rather to write down my impressions and recollections as I remembered them. The book bears out what I have also observed since returning to Melbourne in October 2002 (and attending several speech nights), that the school has flourished in the 60 years since I left it and is still an outstanding school, especially for its academic standards and its encouragement of music.

Bibliography

Gregory, Alan, *Strong Like Its Pillars: Melbourne High School 1905–2005, 2005.*

6

How I Became an Economist

My Wise Father Said No

At Melbourne High School, my favourite subject was history—British History and European History (two separate subjects). If I were to go to university, I thought I would do history. But my wise father said, "No. You should do commerce. You can read history in the evenings". And that is what I have been doing since. My father believed, rightly, that I could get a better job with a commerce degree. He painted a picture of joining a large company, and then gradually rising in it, and making a good living. He was concerned, on the basis of his hard experience, with survival and not enjoyment.

The commerce degree turned out to include a large amount of economics. That is how I got into economics. I can thank my father for that. Of course, I had no idea what an "economist" did, and in any case, becoming an "economist" was not part of my early vision. In my last year at Melbourne High School (1945) I took economics but was not excited by it. The only book that I remember and liked was Copland's *The Australian Economy*, which dealt very clearly with current issues that interested me. As a fanatic newspaper reader, that taste has never left me.

© The Author(s) 2017
W.M. Corden, *Lucky Boy in the Lucky Country*, Palgrave Studies in the History of Economic Thought, DOI 10.1007/978-3-319-65166-8_6

The curriculum of the Commerce School at the University of Melbourne had been, essentially, shaped in 1925 by its founder, Douglas Copland, and the large amount of required economics reflected his influence.

In the first year (1946), I had to take accounting, commercial law, economic geography, and economics, Benham being the textbook for economics. I loved geography, and was utterly, hopelessly, bored by the first two subjects. From the second year, one could specialise. I learnt a lot of economics, especially from a course on industrial organisation taught by Doug Hocking. The two books that I remember and that have influenced me in later years are *The Economics of Imperfect Competition* by Joan Robinson and *The Economics of Welfare* by Arthur Pigou.

My very first published academic article—on newspaper economics— was influenced by the partial equilibrium theory of the firm learnt from the first book, while the underlying theory of my 1974 book, *Trade Policy and Economic Welfare*, was influenced by Pigou's book. Incidentally, many years later, I supervised Rob Hocking, Doug's son, in his Oxford PhD. Sadly, not long after returning to Melbourne, Rob died.

I was strongly influenced by the message which Richard Downing brought from Cambridge that Keynesian economics would ensure that there will not be another depression. I even wrote an article in a student journal about this. I did not really understand Keynes' *The General Theory* but, after I finished the course, I learnt the basics of Keynesian economics from an excellent American text, Dillard's *The Economics of John Maynard Keynes*. At the Honours courses, I was inspired by the enthusiasm and interesting ideas of a Canadian Visitor, Benjamin Higgins.

In the fourth year Honours group (graduating in 1949), there were five of us who got a first-class honours degree, namely Graham Tucker, Sam Soper, Alan Boxer, Russell Mathews, and me. Thereafter, Russell (an ex-serviceman) became a secretary or assistant to Douglas Copland, who was working in a senior official position in Canberra. Tucker, Soper, and Boxer got junior academic positions at Melbourne or elsewhere. I don't think the powers-that-be thought of me as a future academic, possibly because I was rather shy. In my case, Donald Cochrane arranged a position in the management and research side of a major Melbourne newspaper, *The Argus*, which had just been taken over by an English company. This fitted in well with my lifelong interest in newspapers, and possibly becoming a journalist.

I had close contact with several junior members of the faculty, namely Donald Cochrane, Doug Hocking, and Jim Cairns (later a Labor Party politician). I also had some contact with Joe Isaac, who returned from overseas in my last year, and we became lifelong friends. My relationship with Doug Hocking after I left the university was continuous and close, and his course probably had the biggest influence on me, heavily influencing the thesis for my master's degree on "The Economics of the Australian Press", which I wrote as a spare-time activity while I was working at *The Argus*. Also, I had regular contact with the economics tutor in Queens College, Philip Haddon-Cave, who later had an outstanding career in the British Colonial Service, especially as Financial Secretary in Hong Kong.

My master's thesis on the Australian press was mostly historical and descriptive. Later, it attracted the interest of some Australian political scientists, notably Henry Mayer, who had been my coeditor of the 1949 *Melbourne University Magazine*. But there was actually an important by-product of this thesis. This was a short theoretical article entitled "The Maximisation of Profit by a Newspaper". This article turned out to play a significant role in my early academic career. It contained some simple diagrams, influenced by Joan Robinson's *The Economics of Imperfect Competition*. Above all, it was quite original. It analysed rigorously the special case of one kind of multiproduct firm, that is a newspaper producer. In later years, much of my writing analysed real-world issues or episodes, and especially aimed at simplicity of exposition with the help of diagrams. This article, which I dreamt up in 1951 while sitting in the big Reading Room of the Melbourne Public Library, foreshadowed my particular abilities. I think it made a favourable impression on both James Meade and Harry Johnson. It was published in *The Review of Economic Studies*, 1952–1953.

How I Overcame a Disability and Became a Teacher

It was while in London as a British Council scholar that I learnt to overcome a disability. Perhaps it was not a disability, but just a weakness, a natural shyness.

During my time at Melbourne High School, at the University of Melbourne, and Queens College as a student, and many years after, I could not conceive of myself standing up in front of a large (or only small) crowd and speaking. I could not possibly be a university lecturer. Nor did I want to take a prominent visible role in any social or political occasion. I was born not to be a leader. In my activities in the founding of Melbourne University's ALP Club (a breakaway from the more-left-wing Labor Club), I always preferred a back-room role. I was just shy and also influenced by an inferiority complex as a non-British immigrant. Nevertheless, as a member of a large audience in a class, I always studied carefully the virtues and faults of the speaker's technique. If I had been offered a junior academic position after graduating I would have had a problem and perhaps tried to avoid it. And I could not have become a schoolteacher and certainly never a headmaster.

As an academic, I would eventually have to teach and thus need to overcome this disability.

While in London, I received the British Council scholarship to study at the LSE. In London, there was an association for British Council scholars coming from many countries outside Britain. The Council had an annual dinner at which senior members of the Council's board or administration attended. As I remember it, the Chairman (Sir something) made a speech, and then a student was to give the reply. All very formal. For some reason, the Council administrators chose me to give the reply. Possibly, they reasoned that, as an Australian, I would have more command of English than most of the others. Now, that was a challenge for a diffident me and for an Australian brought up on the idea that the English know how to do that sort of thing properly.

So, I carefully prepared the speech in advance. It was tested with my fellow residents at the LSE student residence (Passfield Hall). I learnt it by heart. I had a tiny card giving the first word of each sentence, just in case I forgot something. Perfect preparation. I spoke slowly, since for many years I had observed that good speakers speak slowly. I made sure I did not fiddle with my hands. I looked directly at the audience. Years of study of the right technique came in useful.

Every bad habit that I had observed over my years of study, I avoided. Later, one of the Sir somethings said to me that *he wished he could speak like me!*

Now I knew I could do it, at least with careful preparation. But a few years later, there was to be another awe-inspiring occasion.

In 1958, I returned from London to the University of Melbourne, to take up my first teaching appointment. Before teaching term started, I had to give a public lecture at the Economic Society of Australia (Victorian Branch), held in the University. All my former teachers were in the audience. The topic was "Australia and European Free Trade". Of course, there were no Sir somethings in the audience, but one does hold one's teachers in great respect. So, again, careful preparation was needed. This time, of course, the performance would be a lot longer than at the British Council.

I knew that one should not read a lecture, however long. Only an outline was needed, so as to ensure that I covered all points without forgetting. I put the outline in my breast pocket. And I prepared and rehearsed, of course. I also took a folded blank sheet of paper, so as to make notes in answer to questions afterwards. I strode on the platform looking calmly at the audience, held firmly on to the podium (no fiddling), and pulled out my notes, and put them in front of me. But I happened to pull out the blank sheet of paper. I felt I should not fiddle to get the main sheet in front of me with the summaries of the lecture, so I just spoke. Afterwards someone said to me "Max, you never looked at your notes".

Well, this showed that I could do it. Only careful preparation was needed. And remember. Speak slowly! It also helps to repeat your main messages.

Bibliography

Copland, Douglas, *The Australian Economy*, 1931
Dillard, Dudley, *The Economics of John Maynard Keynes*, 1948.
Robinson, Joan, *The Economics of Imperfect Competition*, 1933
Pigou, AC, *The Economics of Welfare*, 1920

7

Identity: Becoming Australian

It is sometimes said that immigrants have a problem of "identity". I never had this problem. I was a German Jew lucky to have escaped to a foreign country. My task was to "fit in", to do what they wanted me to do, and not to be noticed. That, at least, was at the beginning. I, like my brother, was lucky to be fluent in English when we arrived, and indeed that was a tremendous advantage.

On Not Being a Real Australian

We arrived in January 1939, eight months before the war started, when Australia's immigration policy had been to have immigrants from Great Britain and nowhere else. In 1939, it was not long after the Great Depression, and I suspect that Australians were not even that keen on the British since they could take away jobs. But we, the German Jews, were a humanitarian exception. Many people apparently did not like us coming to Australia, so we had to be as inconspicuous as possible. At the same time everybody we met was very nice. We were known as "reffos", which was short for "refugees".

© The Author(s) 2017
W.M. Corden, *Lucky Boy in the Lucky Country*, Palgrave Studies in the History of Economic Thought, DOI 10.1007/978-3-319-65166-8_7

But "not to be noticed" was important. "Don't speak German on the streets and in the tram. Modulate your voices. Avoid making yourself conspicuous by your manner of dress. Those flat leather portfolios that you carry, those overcoats reaching nearly to the ground may be fashionable in Europe, but in Australia it simply advertises the fact that you are Jewish refugees" (Benjamin, *A Serious Influx of Jews*). That was the helpful recommendation by an official.

I arrived at the age of 11. In the first few years, I was not interested in Australian politics. Anything important happened in Britain, especially when the war began. But after eight years or so, when I was at the university, I began to feel that even though I was not a real Australian, Australia was my country. We were naturalised and thus were citizens. In a sense, being foreign, I was a second-class citizen. The Germans had deprived us of German citizenships, so we were stateless until naturalisation, but even once we received citizenship, I felt that I was not a "real" Australian. I was not aggrieved about that; it was just true.

Later, at the university, I became active—but in an inconspicuous way—in student politics. I became a member of the foundation committee of the ALP Club (ALP = Australian Labor Party), which was a breakaway from the Labor Club, the latter having been dominated by Communists and their "fellow travellers". I wrote the press releases for our new club. This was in 1949, my last year at the university. I had a good friend named Clyde Holding, who was the secretary of the new club. He planned to go into politics and later did so as leader of the Labor Party in the Victorian Parliament and then as a member of the (Federal) Hawke cabinet. I took it for granted that this sort of thing was not for me. But I did have a kind of crush on Mr Chifley, the modest, polite Labor Prime Minister. Furthermore, I joined an ALP branch after I left university. That ended when I left for London, and after returning from London in 1958, I did not rejoin it.

In my last year at the university, 1949, I was coeditor of the very prestigious *Melbourne University Magazine*, my fellow editor being another refugee, a political science student and much older than me, namely Henry Mayer. He was brilliant, exotic, and very confident. In a tribute to him in Rydon et al., *Henry Mayer* I described him thus: "a fully-fledged European intellectual seemed to have dropped from the skies on to provincial Melbourne".

On Becoming a Real Australian Through Multiculturalism

After the war ended, there had been a big immigration programme managed by Arthur Calwell, the Minister for Immigration in the post-war Chifley government (1945–1949). His aim was to increase the population not for humanitarian reasons but for future security. A lesson had been learnt when the USA had saved Australia from the Japanese. Now Australia was transformed with immigrants not just from Britain but from many other European countries, notably Italy, Greece, and Yugoslavia. This was also a period when survivors of the Holocaust, mainly Jews born in Poland, were brought in—with the strong support of Mr Calwell and against the opposition of the usual anti-Semites, including leaders of the RSL (Returned Servicemen's League). Many of the new immigrants had experiences like mine—finding Australians very friendly and yet also (at least in print) meeting a great deal of hostility. The new term of abuse was not "reffo" but "Dago", being aimed at Italians. Of course, at present (2016), they and their offspring have assimilated, like me, and Italian, Greek, Yugoslav (Serb and Croat), Dutch, and Polish names can be found everywhere.

Over the decades, there have been two big changes in immigration policy. First was the end of the blatantly racialist White Australia policy, to which Mr Calwell had been excessively loyal. This change began with the Holt Government of 1966–1967 (which succeeded the long Menzies regime), but was really, almost dramatically, brought about much later by the Fraser government (1975–1983), when a very large number of Vietnamese refugees were brought in. This was a personal achievement of Malcolm Fraser, for which he will have a place in history. It was the definite end of the White Australia policy. The Immigration Reform Group, which consisted of, and sought to influence, academics also played an important role. It advocated an end to all racial discrimination in immigration. Since then there has been a complete change of attitude and policy with respect to Asians, with a large number of immigrants coming from China and India.

What is relevant for my story is the second big change. This is too big a story to expound here in detail (but see Lack and Templeton's *Bold Experiment: A Documentary History of Australian Immigration since 1945*). It refers to the explicit shift in the 1970s to a policy (or perhaps philosophy) of *multiculturalism*. It is recognised, often with pride, that Australia (like Canada) is a harmonious multicultural nation, at least on the basis of the origin of its people. British or Irish origin is not essential for respect. Now there are no second-class citizens. This applies, or should apply, also to people of Indigenous origin whose ancestors, after all, were here first. Immigrants from countries other than Great Britain and (above all) their children or even grandchildren, can be found in high places. One can give a long list of names of politicians, in all the main political parties, as governors of states, ministers, and so on. It is clear that people like me are now *real* Australians. Of course, I should have realised it when in 2001 an AC (Companion of the Order of Australia)—which is the top honour—was awarded to me for my academic work in economics.

I interpret Australian multiculturalism to mean that immigrants are welcome from many different countries or cultures, including Asian, and not just Britain. Furthermore, the government can help new immigrants from various countries to adjust and perhaps overcome initial language problems. It does *not* mean that Australia is, in a sense, a collection of different cultures requiring permanent support for their separate survival in Australia. I can now say: there is no doubt about my identity. I am an Australian—not, of course, the original stereotype of Australian—but an Australian like all the other Italians, Greeks, Jews, Turks, Serbs, Croats, Poles, Dutch, Lebanese, Malaysians, and so on. Immigrants assimilate, especially when they come as children (like my brother and me) but, above all, there is not the same pressure to assimilate immediately after arrival, especially on adults, that was once common.

On Being a German Jew

Yet there is another issue: why I am not just a German or just a Jew? Why do I emphasise that, in origin, I am a *German* Jew.

I have some German characteristics. Actually, Germans would describe them as Prussian. I follow the rules, cross the road only when the light says green, come to meetings on time (or early), and swim in the lane appropriate for my speed, that is *slow*. Israelis call us Yekkes and make jokes about us. Anything I do is meant to be well-organised. This applied, for example, to organising a seminar in Oxford. The other Jews in Europe are *Ostjuden*, who come from the Ukraine, Russia, and Poland (including Provinz Posen which was, for a period part of Germany). The *Ostjuden* are much more likely to be orthodox and observant of Jewish customs. The poverty and persecutions in eastern Europe, especially Tsarist Russia, before the First World War led many *Ostjuden* to move to Germany, where they became a significant refugee minority not, on the whole, welcomed by the German Jews. The latter were, of course, much more assimilated to Germany.

The key historical difference is that the German (and Austrian) Jews were significantly influenced by the Enlightenment while the *Ostjuden* maintained older ways. German Jews tended to be arrogant about *Ostjuden*, something I noticed in my mother and her sisters. This attitude was similar to class distinctions in England. It is worth noting that three of my four grandparents, came from Provinz Posen. Thus, they are likely to have started as *Ostjuden* while their children and grandchildren assimilated to German (or Prussian) ways in Breslau.

I think that many of the Jews in Australia have descended from *Ostjuden*, but, of course, they have had plenty of time to assimilate to Australia. The same applies to Jews in the USA. Incidentally, the family of Australia's most famous Jew, General Monash, came (like my family) from German-speaking Silesia.

My family in Breslau was never seriously observant as Jewish but did belong to a synagogue. As I noted in Chap. 3, my father regarded being Jewish as a burden. My brother, Gerald, used to say in Melbourne that "Hitler made us Jewish", and that was certainly true. I had a bar mitzvah in Melbourne in 1940, and that was it. No more! My parents would go to synagogue at least twice a year, and I would go with them.

On the identity question, I have been conscious of the idea that some of my personal qualities, which have been the basis of my academic success, are essentially "Jewish". I write this with some hesitation. It is not that all intellectuals are Jewish or that all Jews are intellectual (obviously not), but there seems to be some tendency for Jews, on the average perhaps, to be good in the academic arena, whether physics, economics, or other fields. Why is that? There are, indeed, many explanations; for example, several explanations are given in Patai's *The Jewish Mind* (page 338). One explanation that appeals to me is "the religious-cultural tradition of considering learning the highest value".

The Perfect Immigrants?

In Germany, the Jews were enthusiastic and indeed patriotic assimilators to German ways. This was absolutely true of my father and his brother, my Uncle Willy. As a general trend, it goes back to the nineteenth century and the effects of the Enlightenment and the resultant emancipation of the Jews. At first, they were (more or less) accepted, but once the Nazi regime took over in 1933, they were rejected; indeed, "spat out" and forced to emigrate. Not wanted! This is the story of my family. And so, we came to Australia. Here was a country which welcomed us but believed in those early days in immediate assimilation, almost as if by magic. You must look and speak like good Australians and "fit in". And don't take your time! However old you are, you must speak English once you venture out of your home. And (my addition, and certainly not made explicit) if you are the right age, you should marry some lovely local girl—of course, of British descent—as my brother and I did. Well, we German Jews were prepared, and assimilation was our specialty. We were precooked. Were we not the perfect immigrants?

On Being an Anglophile

Apart from being Jewish, German, and Australian, I have yet another identity, one that I shared with Dorothy, my late wife, and also with many friends. And I know that the world is full of them.

I have already written about my eight months at Streete Court School in Westgate-on-Sea in Kent, England. The main memory is that everybody, especially the teachers, were very nice to me. And the fellow students, also. First I went through a strange experience of not understanding anything. But I made fantastic progress and after eight months was fluent in English. It was a good start, never to be forgotten.

I really became an anglophile in Melbourne during my four years, 1942–1945 at Melbourne High School (MHS) and thus during the war. It was the war, and not the school, that mattered in this respect, though the subjects studied at school did matter.

In Breslau, my father used to say: the best thing about Breslau is the fast train to Berlin. In fact anything important always happened in Berlin. Breslau was provincial. Now we came to Melbourne, and it was the same. Melbourne was provincial. The most important thing happened in—no, not Sydney, and certainly not Canberra—in London. Melbourne (or Victoria) was like an English county, 10,000 miles away. Even before the war, this was so: the Australian intelligentsia and the journalists always looked to London for everything. I suppose Melbourne could be compared with a large, provincial city in England. And when the war began, the news was fully dominated by news from London. Who was the most important politician? No not Curtin, or Lyons, or Menzies; it was Churchill, our hero.

In my arrogant way, I felt that Australia had no culture. All that mattered was sport. All culture was British. I would not want to assimilate to Australia but only to the British element of Australia. And that was also the attitude of many more-intellectual Australians.

Everything about England fascinated me. And this was helped by the memory of my school in Kent. I loved looking at pictures of English villages. At Melbourne High School (MHS), I studied British history, and in English Expression was particularly taken by a book of poetry *The Regency Poets: Byron, Shelley and Keats*. Later on came Shakespeare: *Macbeth* and *Hamlet*, especially the first.

I am really describing the so-called cultural cringe attitude of Australian intellectuals, which has been much criticised but was actually justified, at least at that time. It is no more a cringe relative to London than what someone living in Manchester or Leeds feels about London, or someone in Marseilles about Paris—or indeed someone in Breslau about Berlin. It is just that our cultural capital city was somewhat further away. By assimilating to British culture, I was in fact assimilating to Australia, just joining in the national cringe, which came naturally.

In this period during the war, and while I was at MHS, I became fascinated by British politics, especially the Labour Party and the Fabian Society. While I started with reading English Boys magazines, *Champion* and *Triumph*, at some stage, I made a big switch to *The New Statesman*, by then the global bible of social democrats. I bought it weekly. And this settled my future political orientation.

All this was reinforced by the war news which, above all, was about the survival of Britain and dominated radio and the newspapers.

And then there were wonderful English films. And songs "There will Always be an England", "Wish me Luck as you Wave me Good bye", and so on. In far-away Melbourne, I became an English patriot. At school, my closest friend was an evacuee from England.

The anti-Semites, who thought Australia should have been importing Brits rather than Jewish "reffos" in 1939, would have been pleased to know that this child-reffo was really a Brit in disguise, or perhaps a Brit in the making.

If Germany was my first country and Australia my second country, England became my third, and perhaps most important, country. Of course, later on I was to spend nearly five years in London and later still, nine years in Oxford. This reinforced my feeling, and in Oxford, I had the additional pleasure of a very like-minded Anglophile wife.

At this point, I should emphasise that my early years in Australia were completely dominated by the Second World War. I arrived in January 1939, and in September, the war began. It finished in 1945 roughly at the same time when I finished at MHS. Inevitably, I assimilated to Australian—that is, British Empire—patriotism. That was distinct from the effects of my own experiences, which I have discussed.

Here I would like to quote from the memoirs of Sir Edward Woodward, who was just a year younger than me, whom I knew at the university, and who later became a distinguished citizen, including Chancellor of the

University of Melbourne. He writes about his years while he was at Melbourne Grammar (school).

"For many Australians, this patriotism of the war years was the patriotism of the British Empire. In those days I was undoubtedly British first and Australian second. When the war was at its height, I can recall more than once standing strictly to attention with tears in my eyes as the photograph of the King appeared on the cinema screen while 'God Save the King' was played, and early in the war when we Australians sang along with Vera Lynn:

> There'll always be an England. And England shall be free, if England means as much to you as England means to me."

That is well expressed. It is also how I felt, except that my hero was Winston Churchill rather than the king.

What Do We Mean by Identity? The Thoughts of Amartya Sen

In his essay "The Indian Identity", Amartya Sen—the famous Nobel Prize winner and economist—was concerned with the identity of citizens of a thoroughly multicultural, multireligious country. There was one dominant religion, namely Hinduism, the equivalent of the dominant British culture in Australia. All his subtleties are not relevant here; what is relevant is his main conclusion.

An individual (or a group) does not just have one identity, especially not one determined for him or her, either by place of birth or ethnicity, or the religion of the parents. There are many identities, and they can be chosen. Let me just quote from Sen, and I do so because I agree with these conclusions

"We have to resist two unfounded but often implicitly invoked assumptions: (1) the presumption that we must have a single—or at least a principal or dominant—identity; and (2) the supposition that we 'discover' our identity, with no room for any choice. ... Each of us invokes identities of various kinds in disparate contexts ... identity is a matter of discovery rather than choice." The following sentence is also relevant for Australia. "(One) can share an Indian identity without sharing the same religion."

Applying this to myself, the first conclusion is that both the German Jewish identity and the Australian identity should not be overemphasised. There are several identities that I have discovered or developed over a lifetime, which help to explain my life and my attitudes or views. I might ask: Of the many persons I have met and been close to, with whom do I tend to agree? As Dorothy used to say: Are they PLU (people like us)?

The most obvious identity is that I am a western (or orthodox, non-communist) economist, and PLUs certainly include economists from many countries other than Australia or Britain. Some of my closest economist-friends are Asian, for example Indian, Sri Lankan, and Singaporean. But at international conferences, I have met and got on well with economists from numerous countries that I have never visited.

I have friends everywhere. When I visit Canberra, I stay with a Sri Lankan couple, Premachandra Athukorala and Soma, or with Australian Bob Gregory and his Chinese wife, Meng. When I visit Sydney, I stay with Garry Pursell, an Australian, and Astri, his Norwegian wife. When I visit France, I stay with an Irish couple, John and Jackie Martin. When I visit Switzerland, I stay with Henryk Kierzkowski and his wife, Djidka, both Polish, and when I am in England, I stay with John and Jane Black, both (obviously) English. And they are all PLU!

Politically I am centre-left, which would include liberal in the American sense and social democrat in the European sense, and perhaps ALP or Green in Australia, with strong sympathy for "small L Liberals". And then there is the Anglophile identity, which I seemed to share not only with my late Australian wife and my late English-educated brother but also with friends educated in a British way in countries that were once part of the British Empire (notably India and Sri Lanka). Of course, it includes most of my many British friends. And there is no doubt that I share certain attitudes—notably European liberal or social democratic views—with persons educated as central European Jews. This is not a complete list. What is clear is that religion simply does not feature in these lists.

What About Patriotism? Am I Proud to Be an Australian?

So far, I have dealt with the issue of an immigrant, like me, being accepted by the receiving—hopefully welcoming—country. In my case in Australia that took very little time. But there is another aspect, namely the country being accepted by the immigrant. Have I become an Australian patriot, or, at least, am I proud to have acquired some Australian characteristics? Furthermore, does patriotism require me to support the policies of my (Australian) government?

This is a big and ancient subject, which is popular among Australian conservatives. I am pleased and proud when a foreign visitor praises Melbourne. I love showing visitors around. This, indeed, has happened often in recent years (2010–2017). I am pleased when my government does something moral, such as welcoming refugees (like me),and am particularly upset when my government does something nasty, such as the treatment of asylum-seekers, who, unwisely, arrive by boat without a visa. It is even worse when such policies have public support. Patriotism, as I see it, leads people to caring more about what their own government and fellow citizens do than what others do. In that limited sense, I am an Australian patriot. But I don't think that a patriot must always support the government of the day. But that is so obvious, I shall not pursue this subject further.

There is another aspect. Is there an international advantage to being an Australian or acquiring Australian characteristics? For me, in a very limited sense the answer is yes. Here is a case: When teaching outside Australia—in Oxford and later at SAIS in Washington DC—I noticed that my relatively casual or friendly Australian style made me a more effective, or more-friendly, teacher. It was a plus to being an Australian and effectively a sign of my assimilation. This observation possibly makes me more of a patriot!

Bibliography

Patai, Raphael, The Jewish Mind, 1977

Benjamin, Rodney, *A Serious Influx of Jews. A History of Jewish Welfare in Victoria,* 1998.

Lack, John and Jacqueline Templeton, *Bold Experiment. A Documentary History of Australian Immigration since 1945*, 1995.

Sen, Amartya, *The Indian Identity*, in *The Argumentative Indian*, 2006.

Woodward, Edward, *One Brief Interval*, 2005. (His autobiography).

8

What Happened to the Levy Family?

What Happened to My Mother's Family, the Levys?

How were the various family members affected by the German persecution of Jews? If they escaped the Holocaust, where and why? While this chapter goes beyond my personal story, it is meant to give a systematic picture of how the wider family was affected. How lucky were we compared with many of our relatives?

The following should be read alongside the family tree on page 82.

My maternal grandfather, Max, was born in Bromberg, Provinz Posen, and at some stage went to Breslau. He died in 1914. He had six children, who were all alive in 1933, when Hitler became Chancellor. The oldest two, Erna and Alice, were widows in 1933, and the other four were married (the names of their spouses are in brackets). My mother, Kate, was the youngest. The family tree shows that these six children of Max, in turn, had nine children.

We know from Chap. 1 what happened to Kate, Rudolf, and their boys. All four of us got to Australia via England.

© The Author(s) 2017
W.M. Corden, *Lucky Boy in the Lucky Country*, Palgrave Studies in the History of Economic Thought, DOI 10.1007/978-3-319-65166-8_8

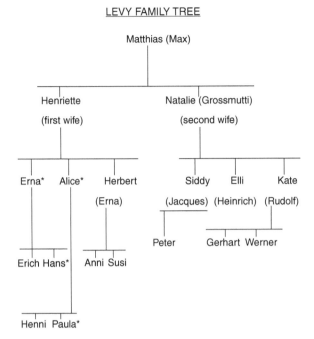

LEVY FAMILY TREE

*killed in Holocaust

Now consider Elli and Heinrich. Heinrich Alter was born in Maehrisch Ostrau, which was then in Austria-Hungary and is now in the Czech Republic. He had a commanding personality, as also did Elli. When Hitler became Chancellor in 1933, Heinrich decided that Germany was not a country he wanted to live in. So he and Elli left Berlin and immigrated to London. This was a brilliant decision! (In England, Heinrich changed his name to Henry.)

Herbert was an accountant in Breslau. He went to Buchenwald with my father in 1938 and got out later than my father. He was injured in the concentration camp. Originally his family of four planned to go to Shanghai but at the last minute managed to get visas for Britain. Hence, they went first to London and then to Glasgow, where they remained for most of the war period. Elli had taken the crucial initiative to obtain the necessary financial guarantees for the family to get visas to Britain.

Siddy and her husband (without their son, Peter) went to Shanghai. Once the war started, this was the only place where one could enter without a visa. They spent the war years there. Life was tough. Elli arranged for Peter (the naughty boy in Chap. 1) to go to school in Kent, England, like me. When the war started, the school moved to Oxford. He spent the war years in England and later became an apprentice in a firm that produced plastic products in Birmingham. Elli and Henry were his substitute parents.

Natalie, mother of Siddy, Elli, and Kate, spent the war years in England, living near Elli and Heinrich (now Henry). This, of course, was arranged by Elli.

Four Were Murdered

What happened to Erna, Alice, and their children? They were living in Berlin. In each case one of the children survived, and the other was murdered in the Holocaust. Both Erna and Alice were widows, and over 50. Their husbands had died many years earlier. The Germans are very good at keeping records. Erna was transported on 17 November 1941 to Riga and presumably murdered there; she was 59 years old then. Alice was transported to Auschwitz on 24 August 1943, and she was 58 years old then. Their names also appear in a book of murdered Berliners, the names of whom are now publicly read out every year in Berlin. (This information came to me from Susi, who lived in Berlin after the war.)

Hans, the second son of Erna, also disappeared, and (so far) I do not know of any record about him. Paula, the second daughter of Alice, also seems to have disappeared. But Erich and Henni survived.

Erich was in his 20s and a young man of initiative. He immigrated to Italy. He kept his surname of Barnass but changed his first name to Enrico. Dorothy, Jane (our daughter), and I met him some years ago in Rome. I am in touch with his Italian grandchildren. Henni obtained a visa to work in London, thanks to Elli, and for many years, she worked as a maid in a well-known hotel, St Ermins. Dorothy and I got to know her well when we lived in Oxford. She died in 1998.

After the War

Peter, Natalie, and eventually Elli came to Melbourne from England (Elli came when Henry died), and Siddy and Jacques came to Melbourne from Shanghai.

As for Herbert's Glasgow family, Anni married, and she and her husband went to a kibbutz in Israel. I am in touch with their three children and families. Her parents later followed her to the kibbutz. Susi went to Berlin. I am also in touch with her. Now (2016) she has a large family and is aged about 90.

Peter married in 1956, I, Max, in 1957, and Gerald in 1959. In all three cases, we have had happy marriages with local "Anglo/Celtic" Melbourne girls, so that at family get-togethers English had to be spoken, not German.

Now, in 2016, most of that generation has passed away, since my wife (Dorothy) and Peter's wife (Vera) have died, as well as Gerald. Only three of us, Peter, Gerald's widow, Peggy, and I are left.

Henni of London, My Lovable Cousin

(This is a slightly condensed version of a note that I wrote in 2006. I have changed the names of the English bank and the law firm [which both don't come out so well in the story] to avoid legal complications. This is a "migrant case study".)

On 21 December 1938, Henni received a letter from the Coordinating Committee for Refugees in London, reporting that the British Home Office had issued her a visa, which she should pick up from the English consulate in Berlin. She had been sponsored for a position with Mrs Gruen of Eton Place, London. I guess this would have been arranged by Aunt Elli.

Henrietta Holz, known as Henni, was born in Berlin in 1911. She was the daughter of Dr Siegfried Holz (who had been a Berlin gynaecologist) and Alice (nee Levy). She had a younger sister Paula (born 1916). Her father died in 1917 at age 47. She was my half-cousin.

Henni was 27 when she arrived in London. She had a job as a housemaid. Later, she worked as a maid in a hotel. I don't know whether she worked in other hotels. I did know that for many, many years, well into her 60s, she worked as a maid at St Ermins Hotel in Westminster, a hotel favoured by politicians and also used by many businessmen. I have the impression that she was greatly appreciated and undoubtedly conscientious. She was still working there when we left Oxford in 1976 to return to Australia and when she turned 65. Possibly near that time she had to retire or part-retire.

I first met Henni in 1953, when I came to London to study. My first impression was that there was some mystery about her. She was just secretive and perhaps even paranoid about revealing much of herself to anyone. She did not tell me that she had been married and divorced in London, where she had lived then for 14 years. (That marriage had left her with the surname of Higgins.) At the same time, she could be blunt. But in time we built up a good relationship, and she certainly missed Dorothy and me after we returned to Melbourne at the beginning of 1958.

Henni never got over the loss of her mother and her sister. They were taken to extermination camps. (See the Levy family history above.) Henni always felt guilty. Such guilt feelings by survivors are common, but she felt she could have done more to get visas for them to come to England. I am sure that Elli would have helped her. But the fact was that she only arrived in England in early 1939, had little or no English, and was extremely insecure. Furthermore, the war started on 3rd September, after which it was impossible (or extremely difficult) to get out of Germany, and certainly impossible to get British visas.

She became quite fluent in English, but what really upset her was that she could not get rid of her German accent. She wanted to become a Londoner, and felt like one, but always—even when she had been in England for more than 30 years—people asked her "Where do you come from?" This question, often asked of immigrants, is rarely meant with hostile intention, but it is hurtful for those who really want to assimilate. In those days, the pressure to assimilate existed in England as in Australia. She would love to have "come from" England.

Actually, Henni was a natural Londoner, perhaps even a cockney, for the simple reason that she was a "big city" type, having been a "Berliner"—and Londoners, Berliners, and New Yorkers are all the same, often funny, enjoying variety, activity, and crowds. She was cheerful even when sad.

Her world was that of central London, where she always lived, first in Belgravia and then near Victoria station. She was both a loner and a mixer. On weekends and other days off, she was happy to go everywhere on her own but would readily talk to strangers, especially waiters. She wanted to be anonymous, and it is easier to be anonymous in a city. For the camera, she would usually put on a glum face because she thought that laughing made her look bad, and yet she had great ability to enjoy herself. She enjoyed eating—perhaps too much—and loved going to hotels and gorging herself on afternoon teas and cakes. We used to take her out with us on day trips from Oxford. She had a great sense of fun. She loved these excursions, especially when it was time to have afternoon tea—with cakes of course. When the food arrived, or became visible at the food counter, her eyes would light up. No inhibitions. When we visited her, she would always lay out a mountain of food but would be really cross if we did not eat enough. But in spite of that, she was self-conscious about her appearance and, as I have said, about her accent.

Henni had nothing to do with the Jewish community and, as far as I know, never went to synagogue. But when she lived in Victoria, she joined a club for seniors run by the local Catholic Church. She considered herself as part of the working class, which is hardly surprising given her job and did not feel comfortable with upper middle-class (St John's Wood) people, and that would have included most German Jews in London. This also meant that she was not comfortable with Aunt Elli, a commanding lady of style, who put a lot of value on good manners and proper appearance.

For much of her time in London during the period when Dorothy, Jane, and I lived in Oxford, Henni lived in a small rent-controlled flat in Belgrave Road. She was endlessly concerned that she would have to move because she thought that the landlord wanted to upgrade the flat. The impression she gave us was that she was poor. We thought she should buy a flat of her own, and I would have been ready to help her financially. She was utterly secretive about her finances and apparently kept much of her money in the bank at low interest. But we had no idea how much she possessed. She resented any questions that I asked. Her prosperous Italian cousin Enrico (Erich), the son of her mother's sister (also murdered by the Nazis), once offered to buy a flat for her in London or elsewhere, but she turned him down. Eventually Henni did move out of Belgrave Road and the Westminster Council provided her with another flat in Gloucester Street, in a fantastic location near Victoria station, and again at a low, controlled rent.

Dorothy, Jane, and I lived in Oxford from 1967 to 1976. By this time, Aunt Elli had moved to Melbourne, so that we were Henni's only relatives in England. Henni visited us regularly on weekends. She came loaded with gifts, mainly for Jane. We called her "Mother Christmas". In the hotel where she worked, guests would often leave behind all sorts of things, including stationery, books, anything, and she would bring these along. Guests would give Henni boxes of chocolates, and these would come also, though Henni would eventually eat much of them. Then she would buy cheap toys for Jane. When we announced that we were returning to Australia, she was devastated, though for several years, we visited London almost every year and spent much time with her. More important, another member of the family, Martin, Gerald's second son, later came to live in London.

Martin came to London in June 1988, at the age of 26. By that time, Henni was nearly 77. After travelling in Europe and elsewhere, he settled down to work in the business of computer sales and servicing in 1990 and finally left London for Australia 11 years later, in 2001. This forthright "Aussie" hit it off with the equally forthright Henni. For many years, she was still secretive and would not reveal her finances to him. He gathered that her savings were poorly invested but could do nothing about that. He took her out for Sunday excursions to Richmond Park and was a regular visitor. Of course, it was never enough for Henni. "Why don't you stay longer?" "Why haven't you phoned?" She was jealous of his girlfriends. A real, touching bond developed between them. Martin has observed that Henni was heavily dependent on a small number of good friends, especially Phyllis Barrett, a very kind Irish lady, who had been a neighbour in Belgrave Road and who, in Henni's last years, regularly did Henni's shopping for her.

Henni died on 27 September 1998. She was 87. For several years, she had been severely incapacitated because of problems with her hip and eventually she could not move out of her flat unaided. Martin, with the help of Phyllis, eventually arranged Henni's reluctant move from her flat in Gloucester Street in Victoria to an old people's home in Wimbledon, which was near the place where Martin lived. Now they arranged her funeral. Well before she died, Henni decided that she wished to be buried, and not cremated, and she bought plot number 4174/H4 at the City of Westminster Cemetery at Milespit Hill.

Henni had made a will which bequeathed almost everything to the Imperial Cancer Research Fund, later known as Cancer Research UK. We have no idea why she chose this particular good cause. Oddly, she left very little to a number of kind persons, mainly recent and former neighbours, including Phyllis, who had greatly helped her in her later years, when she had become quite disabled. (She left a total of 3000 pounds to five persons.) She gave a copy of the will to Martin and deposited the original for safe keeping with the local branch of George Bank. Martin had been managing her money in the last years and knew that, thanks to her extremely frugal living and her German pension, she had accumulated a very substantial amount. He had also invested it for her in more profitable forms than putting it in bank deposits. Her joint executors were a friend, Mary Dunby, and Mr Tony Gedge, a member of the legal firm CMW. They also had copies of the will. The following story may seem slightly surprising, except to those persons who are used to attributing the once-low growth rate of Britain to "characteristic British inefficiency".

In 1993, the will was certified by CMW and subsequently deposited with George Bank. As I have said, Henni died on 27 September 1998. On 15 October, Mark Spash of CMW wrote to Martin: "Unfortunately, George Bank have informed us that they do not hold the original will for Mrs Higgins. It appears that she collected this at some stage in the last 18 months". Martin replied on 23 October that "I doubt that she was capable of retrieving it in the last 18 months". He could have said "She could not possibly have done so". Nothing was heard from CMW until 2 August 1999, when, in a long letter, they explained that probate could not be granted, essentially because the will could not be found. Martin replied immediately in some anger. The will was lodged with George Bank for safe keeping! It was now almost a year since Henni had died. On 11 August, CMW asked who the nearest relatives of Henni were, in case Henni had died intestate. Martin, with the help of his mother and me, supplied the information. There were five cousins of Henni left, these being the nearest relatives as far as we knew.

On 16 September 1999, CMW reported that "George Bank are unable to even estimate when the will was collected and equally cannot confirm whether any document was substituted in its place".

After several phone calls to CMW from Martin, finally they produced some action in March 2000. (This was nearly six months since the last communication.) In a letter to Martin on 8 March 2000, Mr Spash of CMW wrote: "I have referred this matter to one of the Area Managers of George Bank in view of the continued difficulties we have had. In my view we must obtain confirmation from George Bank that they have lost the will rather than that Mrs Higgins withdrew the Will". And a day later, on 9 March 2000, he wrote: "the investigation undertaken by the Area Manager of George Bank has located original Will of 27th October 1993".

A letter of June 2000 reported that probate had been granted. There still seemed to be a long delay after that, but in April 2001, the administration of the estate was concluded.

There was another party to this story, namely the principal beneficiary, Cancer Research UK. When CMW seemed to be so slack in pressing George Bank and getting the matter settled, it seemed to me that Martin should have contacted the principal beneficiary, who really had an interest in getting the money. I am not sure when Martin did this, but it must have been in late 2000. In February 2001, Mr Latham of Cancer Research UK wrote to Martin that he had written twice to Mr Spash of CMW and got no reply, but after a phone call, he had learnt that they were holding 460,000 pounds on Cancer Research's behalf and that all would be finalised once some tax matters were sorted out. After one more reminder by Martin, Mr Latham pressed CMW again, and in April 2001, Cancer Research UK got their money.

Henni's wishes were fulfilled! That was two years and six months after Henni died. The legacy of this apparently rather poor lady was indeed 460,000 pounds. Since her income from working at the hotel, and later her UK pension, must have been quite modest, and her spending was indeed modest, the legacy represented Henni's savings over many years of compensation income from the German government.

Martin and I thought that, in view of the large sum involved, Cancer Research UK should acknowledge Henni in some visible form through a plaque or through some reference in a publication. I sent a background note about Henni at least for their files and suggested wording for a plaque, namely "Donated by the estate of Mrs Henrietta (Henni) Higgins, born in Berlin in 1911. Came to Britain as refugee in 1939, died in London 1998". As a result, plaques with the suggested inscription have been put on four pieces of equipment, located in the organisation's Equipment Park and other places. I have photos of the machines somewhere. In addition, their magazine *Target Spring* 2003, No. 3, contained the following passage in an article about "Legacy Administration":

> So what motivates someone to leave money to cancer research at the end of their life? Patrick Latham of Legacy Administration believes that many donors have known loved ones who have died of cancer. Yet motivations are not always clear, and it still surprises him that five in six donors have no previous known connection with the charity.
>
> This includes remarkable individuals like Henrietta Higgins, who left over 460,000 pounds to the organisation last year. Henrietta came to Britain as a Jewish refugee in 1939, having lost her mother and sister to the Nazis. With no children of her own, she lived a frugal existence, never spending a penny of her compensation money from the German Government. The reason she left almost all she owned to the charity remains a mystery to this day.

Sources

The information about Erna and Alice, who were transported from Berlin and then murdered in the Holocaust, was obtained by my cousin Susi (who lived in Berlin after the War). Susi had obtained official documents, and also had information about her family's experience, especially those of her father, Herbert. The information about other members of the family in the text and the family tree was obtained either from Kate (Mutti) or directly from the various family members, many of whom finally settled in Melbourne.

9

My Lucky Year

In addition to leaving Germany and going to Australia, there were two other lucky events in my life, and both actually happened in 1952. This was the year I met Dorothy, my wife of over 50 years. This transformed my life and gave me a wonderful companion. It was also the year when I found out and applied for a British Council scholarship to study in London. This laid the foundation for my long career as an academic economist.

Thus, 1952 for me was the year of two big turning points in my life.

The British Council Scholarship

In late 1951, I finished working for *The Argus* and became a junior economist at the Commonwealth Department of National Development, based in Melbourne. While at *The Argus*, I was working in my spare time on my University of Melbourne master's thesis, "The Economics of the Australian Press". I did this after work, sitting in the Melbourne Public Library. As a by-product of that thesis, I wrote a short theoretical paper entitled "The Maximisation of Profit by a Newspaper".

This by-product had significant consequences. In early 1952, it led me to visit and ask Professor Wilfrid Prest, the head of the Department of

© The Author(s) 2017
W.M. Corden, *Lucky Boy in the Lucky Country*, Palgrave Studies in the History of Economic Thought, DOI 10.1007/978-3-319-65166-8_9

Economics at the University of Melbourne. How could this paper be published? Perhaps it could be published in *The Economic Record*, the principal Australian economics journal?

Professor Prest glanced at the article, with all its diagrams. He said that he was shortly going to England and would show it to Ursula Hicks, who was an editor of the relatively new English journal *The Review of Economic Studies*.

Then he asked me what I was going to do next. I said I would go to London in time for the Coronation—as vast numbers of young Australians were all planning to do at that time. I would get leave without pay from the Public Service.

Then he asked a fateful question: Why not study? Go to the London School of Economics (LSE)? He suggested that I apply for a British Council scholarship. I would have to apply soon and propose a study programme. I pointed out that I was in the Public Service and had not thought about further study. And then he mentioned that the scholarship might pay for my travel and living expenses. My ears suddenly pricked up. This was a Thursday, and I would have to make an application by Tuesday. I followed his advice and did put in an application in time. I defined my area of interest as "transport economics". This was because I had been reading about the economics of Australian transport, particularly as it applied to the development of the manufacturing industry, which was the special concern of my Department.

How I Met Dorothy

I had originally intended to go to London in 1952, but then, sometime in 1952, a car hit me while I was crossing Russell Street at the corner of Bourke Street, in central Melbourne. My right leg was broken, and because it was the tibia it took nine months to heal. For six months, I was in plaster—endlessly scratching and walking with crutches, and for another three months, I was limping with (metal) callipers. My trip to London obviously had to be postponed.

After some weeks, I went back to work in the department—at first on crutches of course. I learnt to handle these, and especially to master steps and various entrances.

Once I was in callipers (metal supports, replacing crutches), I was mobile again. It was time to get social.

One evening, I went to a YHA play-reading. The Youth Hostel Association (YHA) was a social club consisting mainly of folks in their 20s, who had plans to go overseas (usually to London) for a year or so. Both Gerald and I were members; he was in the skiing group and I in the cycling one. They also had a play-reading group perhaps for the less athletic types. And there was a monthly meeting for all members, held in a large meeting room that was part of Flinders Street Station, facing Flinders St. Every time I walk along this busy street in central Melbourne, I think of this occasion, when I first met Dorothy. The play was Oscar Wilde's, *The Importance of Being Earnest*. I did not participate but just listened. One very good-looking young lady spoke beautifully, with an accent more English than Australian.

That was Dorothy. We were introduced by a mutual friend, and a few days later, we went to the cinema or the "pictures" together (the Regent Theatre in Collins Street). I had to have an aisle seat to stretch out my bad leg. We saw an English film, and, in addition, a short preliminary film about Canterbury. I mentioned that I had been to this famous cathedral town in Kent since I had gone to school close by, and this—Dorothy told me later—greatly impressed her since she loved all things English and had no greater desire than to go there.

I was booked to leave for London in April 1953, and I heard nothing about the progress of my scholarship application before I left. So I paid for my journey, as planned originally. Much later, after I had spent six weeks in France, and then was living in London, earning some money with private tutoring, I got the news that I had been awarded the scholarship and also admitted to the LSE.

To finish this story, Dorothy came to London in 1955, and we were married on 1 June 1957 in Hampstead Registry office. Aunt Elli, who played such an important role in my earlier life, was there and took care of the wedding cake. Before the wedding, we phoned our two families in Melbourne from her home.

In my 44 years as an academic, beginning in 1958, Dorothy and I were together in Melbourne, Canberra, Oxford and Washington DC, and several shorter periods in London, with interludes in Singapore, Stockholm, Florence, and Cambridge (Massachusetts).

One might reflect: Suppose I had not had that 1952 accident. I would not have met Dorothy, and possibly I would not have known about the British Council scholarship and so re-entered academic life. These were two of the biggest turning points in my life.

Part II

Being an Academic Economist

10

The London School of Economics

I arrived in London in May 1953 and went to see the Coronation
Procession on 2nd of June 1953 at Piccadilly, with the Green Park behind
me. Then I went to France for six weeks, staying a little more than a week
in Tourrettes-sur-Loup (in the south of France) with Aunt Elli and Henry.
They were then living partly in this delightful historic town and partly in
London. Sometime after that I was informed that I had been awarded the
British Council scholarship, and then was admitted to the LSE. In
October 1953 (or possibly earlier), I started at the LSE.

My supervisor was to be James Meade. How did that come about?

While I was in the Department of National Development in
Melbourne, I had to write regular reports about the world economy, or at
least those aspects relevant to the department. My main source was *The
Economist*. This was the time of the Korean boom and slump and big
terms of trade shifts and balance of payments problems for Australia. It
was all very mysterious to me since I had never been taught international
macroeconomics properly, if at all. Then I came across a book by James
Meade, published in 1951, *The Balance of Payments*. It was heavy going
but seemed to make everything clear. I started it in Melbourne but really
dug into it in London. I remember sitting in Regents Park in summer

© The Author(s) 2017
W.M. Corden, *Lucky Boy in the Lucky Country*, Palgrave Studies in the History of
Economic Thought, DOI 10.1007/978-3-319-65166-8_10

1953 studying it carefully. Then I discovered that Meade was a professor at the LSE. I requested from the Secretary for Graduate Studies at the LSE, Miss Bohm, that I study under Professor Meade. "That will be difficult, but perhaps he will see you." And he did. And he agreed to take me. And that is how I embarked on my lifelong specialty of international economics. I dropped transport economics as my field and replaced it with international economics.

About this time, my newspaper article was published in *The Review of Economic Studies*, without a word changed from my original submission. This may have been decisive in James Meade's decision to take me on. And something of later significance must be added. An associate editor of *The Review of Economic Studies* was Harry Johnson, and he had refereed my article. Hence, when I first met him later, he knew of me already.

James Meade: Great and Modest

James Meade was indeed a great man., At the age of 29, he was teaching in Oxford and published a book called *An Introduction to Economic Analysis and Policy*, which clarified the debate about the Keynesian revolution. Indeed, it was published about the same time (1936) as Keynes' *General Theory*. It was a great success. He also was responsible (with Keynes' Cambridge colleague, Richard Kahn) for developing the Keynesian multiplier. Thus, he was one of the earliest Keynesians. During the war (1940–1945) he became a member of the Economic Section of the (UK) Cabinet Office, and worked closely with Keynes, and he was the director of the Economic Section from 1945 to 1947. He had enormous influence: first on the construction of the UK national accounts and then on discussions (led by Keynes) about the post-war monetary system, leading to Bretton Woods. But, above all, he produced the basic document (submitted by UK authorities) for a Commercial Union on which the eventual International Trade Organization and GATT were based. By the end of the war, he had not even turned 40. He also wrote the first draft of the Full Employment White Paper (1944), which (among other things) advocated countercyclical variations in social security contributions. After he left the Economic Section, he then spent ten years—

from 1947 to 1957—at the LSE as Professor of Commerce with special reference to international trade. When I first met James Meade at the LSE in 1953, all the wartime and post-war achievements were behind him.

The Theory of International Economic Policy: Two Great Books

During the ten LSE years, Meade wrote the two volumes of *The Theory of International Economic Policy,* for which he received the Nobel Prize in 1977. He shared this with Bertil Ohlin. The first volume, *The Balance of Payments,* was published in 1951, and it was through studying this volume that I had become familiar with his work and indeed become a fan and wanted to be his student. He was working on the second volume, *Trade and Welfare,* while I was at the LSE, and I had the privilege of being allowed to read the proofs around 1956. Both books had a big influence on my own subsequent writings. They were highly original, and he told me that his thinking on which these books were based was greatly influenced by his many discussions with Maynard Keynes.

Meade as Supervisor

My first impression of James Meade was that he was extremely polite and modest, indeed the essence of an English gentleman. As my supervisor, he would read a thesis draft without delay and make modest suggestions for improvement in an almost apologetic way. From his style one would not know, or even guess, his record of being undoubtedly a major figure even then in British and indeed world economics, especially on British economic policy.

When I was first interviewed by James Meade in 1953, he could have been surprised to find that even though I wanted to work in the area of international economics, I did not seem to have read anything on the subject, apart from his book *The Balance of Payments* and the basic

Kindleberger textbook. Indeed, it had been a gap in my University of Melbourne education. So he suggested two books, namely Haberler's *The Theory of International Trade* and Viner's *Studies in the Theory of International Trade*. In my later career, when living in Washington DC, I had the good fortune to get to know Gottfried Haberler closely. I have also had correspondence with Jacob Viner.

My PhD Thesis

I had been interested, as indeed also later, in the economics of immigration, and especially an Australian paper, Karmel's *The Economic Effects of Immigration*, which focused on the effects on the balance of payments. So eventually my thesis topic became "Population Increase and Foreign Trade".

I spent much of the first academic year reading widely, both on trade theory and on demography and population issues. Most important, I became familiar with the pioneering theoretical writings of Harry Johnson on the effects of growth on the terms of trade, especially as represented by his article "Economic Expansion and International Trade (1955)". My own work would have to be within the Johnson framework and also make use of the analysis about population changes in Meade's *The Balance of Payments*. Furthermore, I was completely engrossed or captured by Meade's *A Geometry of International Trade*.

In the summer of 1954, I made a start on the thesis. The LSE owned a manor house in Bramhope, near Leeds, not very far from the Yorkshire Dales, and I went there on a kind of working holiday, playing tennis and going walking at the end of the day with a fellow student (but not of international economics) by the name of Winyu Angkanarat, a Thai, who was also working in the same way. In our walks, we educated each other about the history and politics of our two countries. Hence, I am very knowledgeable about Phibun and Pridi and related matters, which was useful when I visited Thailand in 1961.

The LSE system was that initially one was admitted to a master's degree programme. Presumably if one showed only limited progress, one would get only a master's degree. In my case that would be my second master's degree, the first one being from the University of Melbourne for my "The Economics of the Australian Press" thesis. Once one had shown good prospects, one was transferred to the PhD programme. After I arrived at the LSE and discovered how brilliant and apparently confident the other students were, I wrote to my parents and warned them that I would just get a master's degree, and that, of course, was no problem, even though I already had such a degree. When I returned from my summer in Yorkshire and showed the written result to Meade, he said that I would be transferred to the PhD programme. So the first hurdle was crossed.

Later, the thesis was examined by two persons, oddly, the supervisor (Meade) plus an outside examiner, who inevitably was Harry Johnson. They had no difficulty, and no criticisms, and passed me readily. Later I condensed the main results of the thesis—with the key Meade diagram and some mathematics—into a fairly elaborate article published in *Oxford Economic Papers* in June 1956,

Reflecting on this thesis, I am impressed by the clarity of my exposition. That has turned out to be my "comparative advantage".

On the other hand, this thesis is boring. It is far too taxonomic. And there is clearly a gap. Even though I emphasised several times my original purpose, namely "the effects of population growth (or immigration) on trade, or perhaps the terms of trade, in the special case of Australia", the analysis is never directly applied to this case. Some empirical evidence is required. Hence, on rereading the thesis now, I am not impressed!

My Thesis as Training for Dutch Disease Theory

About 25 years after I wrote this thesis, the issue of "Dutch Disease" arose. See Chap. 14. This became a current issue for many countries, notably for Australia and the UK. It did involve general equilibrium multiproduct modelling of the kind I did in my PhD thesis. Notably the much-cited Corden-Neary article (1982) on Dutch Disease involved this kind of analysis. The thesis has thus been an excellent training for me. It made it possible to conceive many years later what turned out to be my most-cited article ever, helped by mathematical modelling by Peter Neary. My somewhat boring taxonomy at the LSE was thus a most useful beginning for an important and very interesting applied exercise many years later.

Two Articles Published

I wrote two articles in the area of tariffs and protection, and both were published in 1957. I was getting interested in this area while still at the LSE, even though my thesis was not yet finished. When I returned to Australia, protection became my main field. The second article was an elaboration of a point in Meade's *Trade and Welfare* and was the first article of mine that really made an impact. Meade had encouraged me to shorten my first version. But it was the article on the cost of protection that, in the longer view, was the important one. The two articles are listed below:

1. "The Calculation of the Cost of Protection", *Economic Record*, May 1957
2. "Tariffs, Subsidies and the Terms of Trade", *Economica*, August 1957

New Friends

Harry Johnson: My Patron-Saint

It was in 1954 that I met Harry Johnson at the annual Oxford-Cambridge-LSE joint seminar, a seminar that he had actually initiated. He was then a professor at the University of Manchester. He was a Canadian and (amazingly) only four years older than me. He dominated academic international economics for many years and rose like a meteor in the 50s. He was famous not only for surveys that guided the development of international and monetary economics for many years and for particular policy-oriented and theoretical articles he published but also for the incredible number of those. My own LSE thesis was heavily influenced by his specific writings on growth and trade. There was also his inveterate conference-going and networking. He had a strong, almost puritanical belief in the responsibility of academics to their profession.

Harry had already known about me, because he was the associate editor of *The Review of Economic Studies*, when they reviewed my article "The Maximisation of Profits by a Newspaper (1952)". Now we got to know each other and, above all, he ended up being an examiner of my LSE thesis, which drew heavily on his work. From then on, Harry fostered my career, notably in getting me in 1966 to apply for a senior position in Oxford.

Harry died prematurely in 1977.

John Black: A Loyal Friend

John has been one of my closest and long-standing academic friends. We first met at the Oxford-Cambridge-LSE joint seminar in 1954, when he was a student at Nuffield College and I at the LSE. Apart from Harry, he seemed the only one who understood the growth-and-trade paper I presented, and, indeed, he later had a paper in the *Review of Economic Studies* on the same subject, a very good paper. He seemed incredibly bright.

Later, he became a Fellow of Merton College, Oxford, and from there he went on to become a professor at Exeter University. John left Merton before I came to Oxford, and in 1996, he moved to Aberystwyth where his wife, Jane, got a Chair. We met regularly during our visits from Canberra, and later Washington, to Oxford. He and Jane retired to Wivenhoe, near Colchester, in 2005, and I stayed with them for a week in 2012.

He was unusual and very bright. He enjoyed commenting on and even proofreading other people's writings. He read drafts and proofs of several of my books and commented in detail, often on small points. He did the whole of my book *Protection, Growth and Trade*, for which I arranged that he be paid. He was one of several Oxford people who seemed much brighter than me but perhaps less committed to (what Kindleberger called) *Sitzfleisch*—a willingness to sit and write for long periods. I feel I owe a lot to John, a devoted and unselfish friend, since he stopped me from making mistakes in print.

I thanked him in the prefaces of five of my books, *The Theory of Protection*; *Trade Policy and Economic Welfare*; *Inflation, Exchange Rates and the World Economy*; *Protection, Growth and Trade*; and *Economic Policy, Exchange Rates, and the International System*.

Three Fellow LSE Students

It was customary at LSE that new graduate students should present a paper at the Robbins Seminar. This was an awe-inspiring occasion because Lord Robbins was awe-inspiring. The first of our group to present a paper was Kelvin Lancaster. He presented a critique of a theoretical paper in the *Review of Economic Studies*. I don't remember the details, but the performance was brilliant. He used some simile but I have forgotten the details. Robbins was amazed, and so were we all. This student had just come from Sydney and had obtained a first degree in economics as a London external undergraduate student. But he had a very valuable background. At the University of Sydney, he had obtained degrees in mathematics and in English literature. What a combination! His writing and speaking style reflected, in my view, the benefit of the literature degree. For the whole of my time as a student at the LSE, it was accepted that he was the outstanding chap among us. He was three years older than I was but seemed to have been born mature. His manner was quite modest or, better, reticent. He used to sit in the Common Room not actually smoking but chewing a pipe. He would speak in a careful, considered way.

In his later career, he more than fulfilled expectations. He was appointed to the LSE faculty in 1958 and later held Chairs in Johns Hopkins and then Columbia. He produced at least one important book, *Variety, Equity and Efficiency*, and several major papers that transformed a branch of economics, notably "A New Approach to Consumer Theory (1966)", and "Socially Optimum Product Differentiation (1975)". Sadly, he died in 1999, at age 75. If he had lived, he might have become Australia's first Nobel Prize winner in economics.

In his *Who's Who in Economics* entry he wrote: "My predilection has been to search out neglected weak points in our picture of how the economy works, rather than to join the mass attack on problems catching current attention".

Another outstanding fellow student was **Richard Lipsey**. He came from British Columbia and hence, like me, from the outer edges of the British Commonwealth, though he had an MA from Toronto. I had the impression that he knew far more economics than I did and, above all, he had strong views, already firmly formed, about the nature of economics, that is how it should be done. How could a chap, a year younger than me, also coming from "the colonies" be so knowledgeable? I think he was less respectful of senior economists (Robbins, Meade) than I was, but this did not stop him from being appointed to lecturer and then reader at the LSE.

His early output was very impressive. A bestselling and much translated textbook, *An Introduction to Positive Economics*, came out in 1963. Earlier, there was a joint paper with Kelvin Lancaster, "The General Theory of Second Best (1956)", which turned out to be enormously influential. His thesis was on the theory of customs unions. Looking at his massive output of books and articles since then, I note that his interests have been directed to applied issues and with strong and welcome policy orientation. In later years, he has been Canada's outstanding economist (excluding Harry Johnson from the comparison), with much of his writing oriented to Canadian issues. In a sense, Richard Lipsey had some similarities with me and my work on Australia—but surely, at least early on, he had a lot more confidence!

The other fellow student who became my close friend but who was utterly different from the two I have just discussed was **Tadeusz (Tad) Rybczynski**. He was working for Lazard Bros in the city, and at the LSE was enrolled for and obtained a master's degree. He never held a full-time academic position. In his theoretical work, he stumbled upon something important and yet a very simple theorem, namely one that has come to be known as the Rybczynski theorem. It has become a much-cited standard theorem in trade theory. It just happened to fill a gap in my modelling, and I incorporated it in my thesis. He did his analysis with geometry, and I verified it (surprisingly for me) in mathematics. Generations of students worldwide know his name (even if they can't spell it), and yet he has never written more than one theoretical article in trade theory in his life. His famous article in *Economica* is entitled "Factor Endowments and Relative Commodity Prices" (1955).

Personally, Tad was extremely (and unjustifiably) modest, and I have never been sure that he realised what an impact he had made. Many young academics would love to have stumbled on something like that theorem. Tad was in the Polish section of the RAF during the war. He survived many dangers. He was born in Lwow, Poland. He has actually published several books and many articles, all in the area of finance and banking. He has also held many positions in London, of which, perhaps, the most important one was as chairman of the Society of Business Economists (1962–1975). Another important position was as treasurer of the Royal Economic Society. He died in 1998 (aged 75). I went to London from Washington DC for the funeral. It was extraordinary to see the many London organisations he had been associated with represented on this sad occasion. For me he has been one of the most admirable persons I have known.

Four Visiting Students

There were, of course, many other graduate students in economics, some of whom also attended the weekly international economics (or Meade) seminar. Also, the fame of James Meade attracted students doing degrees in other countries, mainly the USA. Here I mention four of them, all of whom became close friends of mine. In most cases, they came for one year only.

Peter Kenen came from Harvard. He would, in future, write many books and articles in the field of international monetary economics. He wrote a bestselling text on international economics that was widely translated. He was very helpful in getting me invited to The Group of Thirty, to various conferences, and also in editing some of my publications for Princeton or various collected volumes. He was always very busy. Richard

Cooper also came from Harvard. He wrote many books, notably *Economics of Interdependence.* He has held senior State Department positions. Later, he and I interacted on many occasions, notably a World Bank project on developing countries (see Chap. 16). He was a very thoughtful person with an exceptional air of authority. Bob Mundell was a Canadian. He was brilliant, unforgettable, and highly original. He was full of confidence. He became a close friend, and in later years we corresponded and met a lot. He invited me to several conferences, and Dorothy and I stayed with him and his wife in Washington DC, and also in his palace in Santa Columba, just outside Siena, in Italy. He loved arguing and drinking. While at the LSE till 1972, he did outstanding original work on what came to be known as the Mundell-Fleming model, and for which he deservingly received the Nobel Prize. Finally, Tom Klein, an American, was writing a University of Michigan thesis on the "1947 Balance of Payments Crisis of the UK". He became a close lifelong friend. When Dorothy and I lived in Washington DC, and I was working for SAIS (1989–2002) and Tom for the World Bank, we two used to go for Sunday walks together in Georgetown.

Other Students

I was living in Passfield Hall, an LSE residential hall with many students in various fields, most of them not British (except for some Welshmen). Three of them became friends with whom I stayed in contact once I returned to Australia. I met Buu Hoan (Vietnam) again in Vietnam in 1961, where he was working for the Central Bank at the time, and he took me to his home town, the ancient capital Hue. Later, we both had moved to Washington DC, and we met several times. Christian Kuhlo (Germany) and I corresponded about his experiences in Russia during the war. Winyu Angkanarat (Thailand) and I met again in Bangkok in 1961, and he took me to Ayutthaya province, where he was the governor. He has held senior positions in Thailand.

Reflections on My LSE Experience

I was most impressed by James Meade's personality but was intellectually influenced above all by his two outstanding books and the Geometric Supplement.

Making contact with Harry Johnson (as well as with his writings) was a major personal event.

A feature of the LSE period was that I made so many new contacts and friends, from whom I learnt and benefited later. Some of them, notably Kelvin Lancaster and Bob Mundell, were quite outstanding. That really was an education.

I also learnt from writing the thesis, but I can see (in 2016) how it relates to my later work, especially the papers on Dutch Disease. The article actually based on my thesis in *Oxford Economic Papers* 1956 was not much cited, but the later Dutch Disease articles were my most-cited papers (along with the *Journal of Political Economy* 1966 article on effective protection). In retrospect, I feel that the thesis was more successful as training than I had thought.

Much of my spare time in London, until the arrival of Dorothy, was taken up by going to the theatre, one of the great prizes of living in London. But my friend Thomas Klein had also reminded me of an absorbing book that I read not long after I arrived. This was Boswell's *London Journal*, a recently published book that was the first of a famous series. In 1762, James Boswell, came to London at age 22 from far-away Edinburgh. His journey took four days. In London, he sought out eminent persons, notably Dr. Samuel Johnson, and started his diaries. His motive of keeping a diary was "know thyself". I also came from far away, though it took me much more than four days to come from Australia by ship to London, and I was 25, and also somewhat awestruck by the people I met in London. My Dr. Johnson was James Meade, and indeed there was also an important Dr. Johnson in my life. Thus this book and message resonated with me and led me to eventually own and read all the Boswell diaries.

The National Institute

When my British Council scholarship ran out, I joined the renowned National Institute of Economic and Social Research as a research fellow for a two-year period (1956–1967). I was to be the junior member of a two-person team, and our study was titled "The Control of Imports in Post-War Britain". My senior colleague was Margaret (Peggy) Hemming, a former Treasury economist. The institute was a great environment; I got to know not just the current staff but many other British applied economists and officials. The general atmosphere was very friendly, and I met many fine and well-informed people. Christopher Dow was writing a major study of the British economy. Lesley Dicks-Mireaux (later at the Bank of England) became a close friend, as did Peggy Hemming, of course. Through Peggy, I met Ragnar Nurkse (Columbia University), an internationally influential development economist. The location of the Institute was terrific—in Westminster (Dean Trench Street) walking distance from Parliament House and Westminster Abbey. Every evening, after work, I would walk to the tube station in Trafalgar Square with Lesley Dicks-Mireaux along Whitehall. Unforgettable.

Peggy and I produced one theoretical article, "Import Restriction as an Instrument of Balance-of-Payments Policy", in *Economic Journal*, September 1958, and I (with the help of Peggy) produced a longer, more empirical, and policy-oriented article "The Control of Imports: A Case Study" in *The Manchester School*, September 1958.

The theory article made some good points but was far too complicated and not clearly focused. I felt that even at the time. When I went back to Melbourne in 1958, I used its diagram for a much-simpler article influenced by the Swan diagram, namely "The Geometric Representation of Policies to Attain Internal and External Balance" in *Review of Economic Studies*, October 1960, and also published in a Penguin book of Readings edited by Richard Cooper. This became well-known.

The *Manchester School* article (220 pages, including Appendix) had masses of information and could have been a government committee document. It should have been sharper analytically. The two principal conclusions were that "devaluation was unsuited for a crisis with so many temporary elements" and "The main value of the import restrictions in 1952 was probably their 'demonstration effect' in reassuring speculators". It seems to me that these were reasonable—but not impressive—conclusions.

Getting Married!!

In 1955, Dorothy came to Marseilles by boat from Melbourne and then took the train to Paris, where I was waiting. We stayed in Paris for a few days. As it happened, Gerald also joined us, on his way to Munich, where he had work to do for the *Rocla* company. Dorothy and I then took the ferry to London. She had a job arranged at the London office of the ABC (Australian Broadcasting Commission). She was to be secretary to the lady (Mrs. Mason) who arranged for internationally reputed musicians, conductors, and so on to come to Australia. (Dorothy had worked for the ABC in Melbourne.) Before Dorothy came, I used to go to many plays— for which London was famous—but now we went to numerous concerts at the Royal Festival Hall and the Royal Albert Hall, all with free tickets.

On Saturday, 1 June 1957, Dorothy and I were married at the Hampstead Registry Office. The weather was beautiful. The reception was held at the home and garden of my colleague Peggy Hemming and her husband, Francis, in Park Village East, Regent Park. Many of my colleagues from the National Institute were there, as also Dorothy's colleagues at the ABC, including her boss, Mrs. Mason; we also had Tom Klein and his fiancé, Judith; Tad and Helen Rybczynski; John Black; and two members of my family, Aunt Elli and cousin Henni.

We went on a honeymoon beginning at the Ile St. Louis (Paris), and then to Stuttgart (where Dorothy had a friend), Vienna, and Fieberbrunn (a delightful resort town near Innsbruck), and ending in Cologne (where it was very hot).

We then lived for a little while in Dollis Hill (North London) and returned to Melbourne at the beginning of 1958. I had arranged a job in the Department of Economics of the University of Melbourne, specifically in a small department within the larger department.

Bibliography

All the information above, and more, about James Meade, can be found in a long and fascinating article on Meade in the *New Palgrave Dictionary of Economics, Vol 3*, written by David Vines, a Melbourne graduate and later colleague of Meade in Cambridge.

W. M. Corden, "The Control of Imports: A Case Study.", The Manchester School, September 1958.

WM Corden, "The Maximisation of Profits by a Newspaper", *The Review of Economic Studies*, vol. 20 1952–53.

WM Corden "Economic Expansion and International Trade: A Geometric Approach." *Oxford Economic Papers*, June 1956.

WM Corden, "The Calculation of the Cost of Protection", *The Economic Record*, May 1957.

WM Corden, "Tariffs, Subsidies and the Terms of Trade", *Economica*, August 1957.

WM Corden with M.F. Hemming, "Import Restriction as an Instrument of Balance-of-Payments Policy", *Economic Journal* September 1958.

WM Corden with Peter Neary, "Booming Sector and De-Industrialisation in a Small Open Economy", *The Economic Journal*, December 1982.

James Meade, *The Balance of Payments*, Oxford University Press 1951.

James Meade, *Trade and Welfare*, Oxford University Press, 1955.

James Meade, *A Geometry of International Trade*, Oxford University Press, 1952.

James Meade *Economic Analysis and Policy*, Oxford University Press 1936.

Peter Karmel, "The Economic Effects of Immigration", in *Australia and the Migrant*, Australian Institute of Political Science, Angus and Robertson 1953.

Harry G Johnson, "Increasing Productivity, Income-Price Trends and the Trade Balance", *Economic Journal*, September 1954.

Harry G Johnson, *International Trade and Economic Growth*, Allen and Unwin 1958.

John Black, "Economic Expansion and International Trade: A Marshallian Approach" *Review of Economic Studies*, June 1956

Tad Rybczynski, "Factor Endowments and Relative Commodity Prices" *Economica* 1955.

Kelvin Lancaster, *Variety, Equity and Efficiency*, Columbia University Press, 1979.

Kelvin Lancaster, "A New Approach to Consumer Theory", *Journal of Political Economy*, 1966.

Kelvin Lancaster, "Socially Optimal Product Differentiation", *American Economic Review*, 1975.

Richard Lipsey, *An Introduction to Positive Economics* 1963. (also 11 translations)

Richard Lipsey and Kelvin Lancaster, "he General Theory of Second Best", *Review of Economic Studies* 1956.

Richard Cooper, *The Economics of Interdependence*, Columbia University Press 1968.

Boswell's London Journal 1962–63, Frederick Pottle (ed.), Heinemann, London 1950.

11

Australian Tariff Policy and the Theory of Protection

After we returned from London to Melbourne in 1958, my main research and writing was about Australian tariff policy. Protection of manufacturing industry was a hot issue in Australia. Right through my career as an economist, my choice of research topics has been determined by current events and policy issues. This was why I started working on this topic. My analysis of Australian tariff policy was followed by policy recommendations.

In Parts 1 and 2 of this chapter I describe what happened in Australia in this field, and why my talks and writings did have a significant impact on Australian policy discussion and eventually on actual policies.

Part 3 is concerned with a new concept in the area of protection, namely *effective protection*. I did not invent it, but I played a large role in explaining and developing it. It led to one of my internationally best-known articles. It raised many complicated issues, and finally I tried to sort them all out in my 1971 book *The Theory of Protection*, written when I was at Oxford.

Finally, in Part 4 I ask: Is this subject of protection really worth working on any more when it seems that policies of protection have gone out of fashion?

© The Author(s) 2017   **113**
W.M. Corden, *Lucky Boy in the Lucky Country*, Palgrave Studies in the History of
Economic Thought, DOI 10.1007/978-3-319-65166-8_11

In what follows I shall refer to various lectures I gave and articles I wrote on Australian policy. Mostly they have been published in journals, but more conveniently they are all also available in my book, *The Road to Reform: Essays on Australian Economic Policy* (1997).

Making a Difference: Australian Tariff Policy 1958–1967

How It All Began

Before I left for London in 1953, I had discovered the Brigden Report (1929). This report was entitled "The Australian Tariff: An Economic Enquiry". It was written in the 1920s by a group of Australian economists headed by J.B. Brigden. They were working under official sponsorship. The principal conclusion was that tariffs were needed in Australia to employ a growing population.

In addition, the report contained an innovative calculation of *the cost of protection.* I did not really understand the arguments and the significance of the "cost-of-protection" calculations. That was an intellectual challenge. Therefore, in 1955, while I was at the LSE, I worked through it carefully. The result was my first article in this field, namely "The Calculation of the Cost of Protection", published in *The Economic Record* 1957.

Background: Tariffs and Import Licencing in Australia

Australia's tariff history goes back a long way, in fact to protection in the state of Victoria in the nineteenth century. But there was a big increase in protection after the First World War, which was also the time when the Tariff Board was established. This interesting institution was meant to be an independent (but government-appointed) board, with its own staff, that would review all proposals for new tariffs or changes in tariffs and give advice to the federal government. Australia developed a comprehensive system of protection of manufacturing industry by tariffs. By the end of the 1950s, an import licencing system was superimposed on this, being the result of the balance of payments problem that had resulted from the slump in commodity prices when the Korean War boom ended in 1952. At that time, Australia was more protectionist than any other OECD country except New Zealand.

The Adelaide Lecture 1958

In June 1958, not long after I returned from London to the University of Melbourne, I gave a lecture at the Australian and New Zealand Association for the Advancement of Science (ANZAAS) Annual Congress, held in Adelaide. Sections G of these annual meetings were the predecessors of the annual conferences of the Economic Society of Australia. My topic was "Import Restrictions and Tariffs: A New Look at Australian Policy". Essentially, I argued that tariffs should replace quantitative import restrictions (which were then pretty comprehensive), and that tariffs should gradually be made uniform ad valorem. The emphasis on tariff uniformity—designed to minimise distortions within the protected sector—was the really important message, with a big effect on policy. Possibly a further step might be to add export subsidies and eventually replace the uniform tariff and the uniform export subsidies with a devaluation. All this was proposed in the most cautious way, allowing for gradualism, and various qualifications. The focus of the paper was on the desirability of tariff rate uniformity, or a movement in that direction. I spelt out arguments against protection in detail. This lecture made a big impact. It was fully reported in the newspapers and certainly attracted more attention at the Section G conference than any other presentation.

The Logic of Australian Tariff Policy

The next stage in my work was an in-depth study of the logic of Australian tariff policy as it existed, both the logic in general (which was based primarily on the Brigden Report) and the logic of the tariffs in particular—that is the detailed differential system. This had never been done before. I tried to relate this logic to standard economics. An element of the logic was the idea of the "made-to-measure" tariff, a term I did not invent but did popularise. My research was thus empirical but not statistical or econometric. Rather, it was a study of institutional behaviour. My detailed description of "the logic" can be found in chapter 4 of *The Road to Reform*.

I had already been reading Tariff Board reports to get an idea how the members and staff of the Board thought, but tariffs became really important only from 1960, when the whole system of quantitative import restrictions was removed. This was two years after we returned to Melbourne from London. I then studied in detail the processes and apparent logic (insofar as there was any) of tariff-making. This was an important stage in my work. If one is to criticise a system, one has to understand it. Usually there is some "logic" even if it is not the logic that can be found in the professional economics literature. Indeed, there seemed to be no connection between standard economics and Australian tariff "logic", so this was a challenge.

To summarise, the basic logic was as follows. First, the logic in general (originating with the Brigden Report) was to ensure employment of a growing population and thus to make population growth possible. Exchange rate depreciation was ruled out, and, in effect, tariffs took the place of depreciation. Secondly, there was the implicit "existence principle" (my term). Industries or activities would be protected if they came into existence for whatever reasons. They may have come into existence during the First or the Second World War when foreign supplies of goods were cut off, or earlier (in Victoria), after the end of the Gold Rush when there was an employment problem, or indeed as a result of political decisions. Thirdly, the size of a particular tariff rate was determined by the "made-to-measure" principle, which involved the Tariff Board measuring, sometimes elaborately, the cost disability of the industry seeking protection relative to costs of competing industries abroad (mainly Britain). If the disability appeared to be very large, the proposed industry was considered not "economic".

Why Did My Talks and Writings in the 1960s Make an Impact?

The answer to this question may shed some light on the role of academics in influencing economic-policy reforms. I am referring here to my contributions before I left for Oxford in 1967. My last policy proposals were in the 1967 Fisher lecture, which analysed very critically recent tariff policy and also set out a detailed pragmatic programme for the future.

My policy lectures and articles made an immediate impact for four reasons.

Firstly, they were timely. With the inevitable removal of import licencing in 1960, tariffs became really important again, and members and staff of the Tariff Board needed guidance. It was obvious that the existing system, heavily influenced by political pressures, was inadequate. There was a need for principles to guide individual tariff decisions. It was pure chance that the subject I had been thinking about and working on, and that had not been much discussed or studied by Australian academics for some years, was becoming highly relevant at that time.

Secondly, two crucial individuals, Alf Rattigan, who became chairman of the Tariff Board in 1962, and Bill Carmichael, who was his "right-hand" man, held key positions and were prepared to rethink tariff policy and the details of tariff-making. These were two admirable—indeed outstanding—public servants. They were politically skilled and prepared to support major changes if in the national interest. My work filled a need for them in providing an intellectual basis as they worked out their reform proposals. Bill Carmichael was particularly important in this process.

Thirdly, my proposals were pragmatic. I never proposed radical, politically inconceivable changes. I always suggested changes in stages, laid out alternatives, and, above all, had in mind gradual changes. Mostly I made the explicit assumption that the exchange rate would stay fixed, this being the basis for proposing some kind of uniform tariff. This was a most important assumption. I believed it to be realistic but shall come back to it. In retrospect, I believe that I was too cautious and advocated second-best (or worse) solutions.

Fourthly, it helped that I was clearly familiar with the details of tariff-making and did not just rely on general principles. I could not be accused of being an academic who only knew "theory". That was the result of having carefully studied the "logic".

The Vernon Committee

In 1965, the Commonwealth government appointed a committee of economic enquiry to review the Australian economy. It submitted its report in 1966. It was known as the Vernon Committee (after the name of its chairman). Its highly influential deputy chairman was Sir John Crawford. It made extensive recommendations concerning tariff (and other) policy, including two that clearly embodied my ideas. The first was the idea of a tariff "benchmark", as a guide to the determination of tariff levels, and the second was the desirability of tariff rates, including the benchmark, being measured in terms of *effective protection*. The "benchmark" proposal embodied the idea that a tendency to tariff-rate uniformity was desirable: it embodied thus a bias to uniformity. The adoption of *effective protection* was important, and I discuss it later in this chapter. Anyway, whether directly through my writings or through the Vernon Committee, the Tariff Board implemented these recommendations, which represented radical reforms.

Trade Liberalisation By the Hawke Government

I left Australia for Oxford in 1967. The really big changes in tariff policy took place in the 1980s, that is after I left. The changes that happened after 1967 are described in my book, *The Road to Reform*, and also in more detail for the 1970s in Anderson and Garnaut's "Australian Protectionism: Extent, Causes and Effects", 1987.

I returned to Australia (ANU) from Oxford in 1977, but I had no direct role at all in the new tariff policy except that I had provided earlier the intellectual groundwork for the radical liberalisation that eventually took place.

The crucial year was 1988. The Labor government, with Bob Hawke as Prime Minister, was in power. Ross Garnaut (on leave from the ANU) was his principal economic adviser and deeply involved with the new policy. In 1988, the government issued an economic statement that announced a general programme of phased reductions in nominal tariff rates for most imports. In 1991, there was a recession but nevertheless the government announced a continuation of this tariff reduction programme.

All this was remarkable. Australia was coming close to complete free trade.

The background and motivation of these events are discussed thoroughly in Garnaut's *Australia: The Political Economy of Policy Reform* (1994). Here it should be mentioned that the earlier Labor Whitlam government (1972–1975) had also introduced some tariff reductions, though not as radical as the Hawke government. In that case, the relevant economic adviser was Fred Gruen. Garnaut actually describes the whole Hawke government period from its beginning in 1983 (which included financial reforms) and goes deeply into the very interesting political economy of the whole remarkable period. How could something like that happen? Of course, Ross Garnaut himself was an important actor, perhaps second only to Hawke.

Crucial Role of Exchange Rate Flexibility

Exchange rate flexibility played a crucial role in making Hawke's radical trade liberalisation possible. The central point was that a general reduction of tariffs and, even more, their elimination would, on its own, reduce employment in Australia, possibly severely. For such a policy to be acceptable it had to be offset by sufficient depreciation of the exchange rate, which would increase employment by making the country more competitive.

All my proposals in the 1960s had been in the realm of the second-best. I did make it explicit that a first-best policy would involve devaluation of the exchange rate, as part of a movement to free trade. But, in practice, I dismissed devaluation as unrealistic. The exchange rate was fixed. This was part of my pragmatism, which, in retrospect, I regard as excessively cautious.

Now comes the key to the whole process. In 1983, the new Hawke government floated the Australian dollar ($A). The market then depreciated the $A in 1985 and 1986 owing to the decline in the terms of trade.

It would then depreciate further if there were tariff reductions, so the possibility of a first-best policy emerged. The favourable-employment effects of depreciation would offset the unfavourable effects of tariff reductions. This was a precondition for the acceptability of the remarkable tariff reforms of the Hawke government, aiming at the gradual reduction and eventual elimination of all tariffs.

In effect, depreciation came first, and tariff reductions followed. The policy was still pragmatic in the sense that tariff reductions were gradual and preannounced. But the floating of the dollar made a pragmatic and gradualist first-best policy possible. Many of the complications about second-best policy (including the *effective protection* measurement) about which I had been writing, and which had influenced the Tariff Board, became quite irrelevant.

The history of Australian tariff reform and its associated battles, involving at first, above all, the Minister for Trade, John McEwen, and the chairman of the Tariff Board, Alf Rattigan, has been written up in many places. See Rattigan's *Industry Assistance: The Inside Story* and Garnaut's *The Political Economy of Policy Reform*. Much happened during the 1960s, and, above all, later. I reviewed the whole Australian liberalisation process up to the early 1990s in "Protection and Liberalisation in Australia and Abroad" which was my second Fisher lecture.

My Two Contributions to Policy

I now look back and reflect what difference my writings in this field of trade policy reform made.

In retrospect, I made two contributions to Australian policy through my writings, one minor and one major. The *minor* one was to suggest and advocate some improvements in the details of tariff-making in the 1960s, with (a) my emphasis on minimising non-uniformity of tariff rates, as set out in my Adelaide lecture and (b) the switch of measurement from *nominal* to *effective protection*. These were contributions in the short-term world of the second-best limited to the 1960s. By second-best I mean that it was not free trade—the best involved zero tariffs. These second-best changes were brought about partially through the Vernon Report and, above all, through the decisions of the Tariff Board.

My main, *major* or *long-term* contribution was to draw public attention to the costs of protection, the need for tariff-policy reform, and, above all, the need for devaluation or depreciation of the exchange rate if the best outcome was to be approached. My writings in the 1960s helped to change elite opinion and thus made the radical Hawke changes in the 1980s possible. The credit for the big, even dramatic changes must go to Prime Minister Bob Hawke and his principal adviser, Ross Garnaut. But they needed the support of *elite* opinion. As to my role, and that of other academics, this is best summarised in Garnaut, *The Political Economy of Policy Reform*. I quote:

> The change in the climate of elite opinion on protection can be traced to work by academic economists through the 1960s. Economists began to examine closely and to publish studies on the costs of the highly differentiated Australian tariff. At first, the main reform advocated was movement towards a uniform tariff. By the late 1960s, the economics profession was advocating import liberalization with near unanimity and with increasing technical sophistication. ... The new views of the Australian economics profession gradually influenced opinion in the bureaucracy, commencing with the Tariff Board.

Here is a final question about my role on policy: What was my underlying philosophy or motivation affecting my writing on tariff policy in the 1960s? Was I a "neoliberal" or—even worse—"a market fundamentalist"? The brief answer is "no". Rather, as a student I fell under the influence of Arthur Pigou's *The Economics of Welfare*. This book showed how externalities should be dealt with in the presence of market failure using appropriate taxes and subsidies.

I was not opposed to the principle of government intervention. There is surely an important role for governments. But intervention needs to be rational and in the national interest. That is indeed a "liberal" way of thinking, but not what the enemies of so-called neoliberalism have in mind.

Effective Protection

While at the LSE, I devoured books and articles in the famous LSE library. I discovered an article by a Canadian economist named Clarence Barber entitled "Canadian Tariff Policy". It expounded the novel idea of *effective protection*. This is the rate of protection in relation to value added. It is best explained with a formula, but let me quote from the expository article (in the *Journal of Political Economy*, (1966)) which I later wrote about it.

> Ordinary nominal tariffs apply to commodities, but resources move as between economic activities. Therefore, to discover the resource allocation effects of a tariff structure one must calculate the protective rate for each activity, that is the effective protective rate. It depends not only on the tariff on the final commodity produced by the activity but also on the input coefficients and the tariffs on the inputs.

> For example, a tariff on imports of motor car components will reduce the effective protection for the local manufacture of motor cars.

Once I started working on Australian tariff policy, with all its details, I realised that the concept of *effective protection* was quite crucial to understanding the economic effects of Australian protection policy. I recommended that effective protection rates for Australian industries or activities should be calculated by the Tariff Board and that policy recommendations should be influenced by such rates. In particular, the aim should not be to make nominal tariff rates as equal as possible, but introduce effective rates. In fact, the consequence of this line of thought was quite radical.

This led to a transformation of Tariff Board methods and activities, which is owed (as I have already mentioned) to two persons, namely Alf Rattigan, chairman of the board and Bill Carmichael, the development officer, who were really the driving force behind these changes. My policy recommendations—for example the 1967 first Fisher lecture—always included allowance for effective protection aspects. I have written about all of this, and much more, in "Effective Protection and I" in *History of Economics Review*, 2005.

The most widely read of my publications on Australian tariff policy was a lengthy chapter called "The Tariff" in *The Economics of Australian Industry*, a big book edited by Alex Hunter (1963). I had written a long exposition of the effective protection concept in this chapter. An Appendix consisted of various case studies, where I had calculated or guessed at effective protective rates for various Australian industrial activities.

It should be borne in mind that once nominal tariff rates in Australia had become very low owing to the post-1988 Hawke liberalisation process, the effective protection complication became much less important, at least in Australia. As I shall now show, it was another story internationally.

My Most Important Article

In 1964, I submitted an article on effective protection to (Britain's) *The Economic Journal,* which was rejected in 1965. I then sent it to Harry Johnson, who was an editor of the *Journal of Political Economy.* He made many suggestions for improvement, and after being refereed it was published in this journal (see Corden 1966a). Thanks to Harry Johnson, this turned out to be a much better article than the original one that I had submitted to *The Economic Journal.* In fact, it was the most important article (my "Star" article) I have ever published! (Possibly a later article on Dutch Disease outranked it in terms of citations.) Essentially it was about measurement theory, not about policy. It opened up many difficult issues. It had a big effect on my academic reputation.

Effective Protection: An International Boom

While effective protection had its first impact on policy in Australia, as I have described, that came to an end as a result of Hawke regime's trade liberalisation that began in 1988, and that caused, after some years, to bring Australia close to (almost) free trade. A country that has (more or less) free trade does not need to calculate effective protection rates. But this was not the case in many other countries. Protection through tariffs and other devices, notably subsidies and quantitative restrictions, was extremely prevalent in many, indeed almost all, developing countries, notably in Latin America, India, and Indonesia. It was a major feature of the economies of these countries. And this explains the extraordinary international impact of my effective protection article.

In late 1964, before this article was published, I visited many universities in the USA, thanks to a Carnegie travelling fellowship. This was my first visit to the USA. I gave seminars on effective protection. The response was striking, primarily from graduate students writing dissertations on developing countries. Earlier Harry Johnson had also been making presentations on this subject in the USA, and the subject was in the air. These seminar visits by Harry and me, and then my JPE article, influenced the choices of dissertation topics by many students and indeed in the following years many articles worldwide were published, both theoretical and empirical, which resulted from this particular boom.

The various measurement problems or issues that I had raised in my JPE (1966a) article were endlessly analysed, and, more importantly, an opportunity was provided for students to do empirical dissertations of a relatively simple (but laborious) kind, namely calculating effective rates of protection for their own countries. This was connected with the gradual awareness that high protection was a particular feature of developing countries' economies, and a possible cause of their low levels of development. It created an empirical basis for the belief that protection rates were often very high and thus led eventually to the later pressure for reducing protection. Also, the effective protection figures drew attention to the high *dispersion* of effective rates as compared with nominal rates.

In 2003, an outstanding article was published by Greenaway and Milner ("Effective Protection, Policy Appraisal and Trade Policy Reform"), which explored the main issues about the value of the effective protection concept again in detail. Their argument was that effective protection calculations had been very useful in providing reasonable, though not perfect, data for policy appraisal and trade policy reform. They were writing with a thorough knowledge of actual policy development (especially trade policy reform) in developing countries. They noted that empirical evidence of dispersion of effective rates in many countries was particularly important in guiding policy reforms, and that various general equilibrium models could not be adequate substitutes. I regard this as one of the most valuable articles in the field.

I cannot leave this topic without referring to the impact that Harry Johnson and Bela Balassa have made on this topic.

In 1964, Harry Johnson gave a lecture in Geneva on effective protection, later published as Johnson (1965). This was the most comprehensive theoretical paper on that subject up till then. No doubt he had been influenced by the original Barber (1955a) paper, and possibly also my 1963 Australian paper. He dealt with many aspects, including the implications of the concept for trade negotiations. Harry had an outstanding ability to see where the gaps in the field of international economics were, and he played a major role in stimulating the first two big empirical studies of effective protection, namely Balassa (1965) and Basevi (1966).

The late Bela Balassa turned out also to be a major figure in this field. He worked under the auspices of the World Bank. His big, ambitious effective protection project was reported in Balassa et al. (1971). He was crucial in the international dissemination of the concept and of empirical work on developing countries. It is not surprising that the names of Barber, Corden, Johnson, and Balassa are always correctly associated with this concept.

Finally, while at Oxford, I wrote and published *The Theory of Protection* (1971), which sought to consolidate the theory and deal, as far as possible, with the various analytical difficulties, notably the "substitution problem". That was enough for me, though—as a total assessment of work in this field—I would give pride of place to the recent article by Greenaway and Milner (2003).

Is Protection Still an Important Issue?

Large-scale trade protection of the kind that Australia and many developing countries have practised in fairly recent years may be regarded as a social disease. By measuring and analysing it, economists have contributed to reducing the extent of this disease.

Of course, it has not disappeared completely. Indeed, it may sometimes be a second-best remedy for other diseases. And it is still an issue in some developing countries. Furthermore, there are still various kinds of intervention by governments, other than tariffs, and mostly through subsidies, where the protection analysis is still relevant. Hence, the battle continues. A recent example of the battle is an excellent, vigorous exposition of the case for free trade and analysis of the weaknesses of protectionist arguments in Douglas Irwin's *Free Trade under Fire*, 4th Edition, 2015.

Nevertheless, I began to think that the disease was declining and perhaps no longer of great interest. Thanks to Bob Hawke, this was certainly true in the Australian case. Hence, once my book *Trade Policy and Economic Welfare* was published in 1974, I decided to stop working in this field and switch to international macroeconomics. This "switch" took place while I was at Oxford. But the situation changed dramatically in late 2016.

Yes, It Is Back!

The USA elected a President who was a bold, enthusiastic protectionist. And he has his acolytes. *Protection is back! The disease is back!* So, there is more to do and to analyse or resurrect ancient arguments.

Inspired by these recent developments, the central issue is best understood in terms of a concept that I introduced in chapter 5 of my book *Trade Policy and Economic Welfare*, namely the "conservative social welfare function (CSWF)". It is a good explanation historically for the introduction, or for an increase, in protection. The aim of policies is often to avoid declines in sectional incomes.

The justified concern is with income distribution. How can this objective be reconciled with other policy objectives, especially keeping the gains from international trade? The answer is obvious. The essential message would be that, if there are two policy objectives, it is necessary also to make use of at least two policy instruments. The second policy instrument has to be focused on national income distribution. The complaints about the adverse effects of globalisation reflect a failure for the social welfare system in some countries, notably in the USA, to adequately compensate the losers from international trade or indeed from other adverse shocks, such as those created by technological developments.

Bibliography

WM Corden *The Road to Reform: Essays on Australian Economic Policy,* Addison-Wesley 1997.

Most of the articles listed below, if they concern Australia and were written by me, are reproduced in this book of collected articles, as well as having appeared in *The Economic Record.*

W.M. Corden, "The Structure of a Tariff System and the Effective Protective Rate", *Journal of Political Economy*, Vol. 74, June 1966, pp. 221–37.

This is my "star" article, with a high citation record. It is fully reprinted in two of my books of collected articles, namely *Protection, Growth and Trade: Essays in International Economics*, Basil Blackwell 1985, and *International Trade Theory and Policy: Selected Essays of W. Max Corden*, Edward Elgar 1992.

WM Corden, "The Calculation of the Cost of Protection" *The Economic Record* 1957. In retrospect, this was one of my most original, articles, relevant for all countries with protection. It was my first significant article in the 'Protection' area which dominated my work for many years.

WM Corden. "The Substitution Problem in the Theory of Effective Protection", *Journal of International Economics*, February 1971

WM Corden "Import Restrictions and Tariffs: A New Look at Australian Policy", *The Economic Record,* December 1958. This was my "Adelaide Lecture."

WM Corden "The Tariff" in A. Hunter (ed.) *The Economics of Australian Industry*, Melbourne University Press, 1963.

WM Corden "Australian Tariff Policy" (1st Fisher Lecture) Adelaide, 1967.

WM Corden, "The Vernon Report: Protection," *The Economic Record*, March 1966b.

WM Corden *"Protection and Liberalisation in Australia and Abroad" (2nd* Fisher lecture*) Australian Economic Review, Adelaide,* 1996.

WM Corden "Effective Protection and I" *History of Economics Review,* 2005.

Brigden J. B et al., *The Australian Tariff: An Economic Enquiry,* Melbourne University Press 1929

C L Barber, "Canadian Tariff Policy", *Canadian Journal of Economics and Political Science*, 1955a.

Anderson, Jym and Ross Garnaut "Australian Protectionism: Extent, Causes and Effects." Allen and Unwin 1987.

This is an excellent, comprehensive review of Australian protectionism, including its causes and effects, and going back to 1901 and forward up to the 1970s.

AC Pigou, *The Economics of Welfare,* 1920

Clarence Barber, "Canadian Tariff Policy" *Canadian Journal of Economics and Political Science,* 1955.

HG Johnson, "The Theory of Tariff Structure with Special Reference to World Trade and Development", in Johnson, HG and Peter Kenen, *Trade and Development,* Geneva 1965.

Balassa, B. "Tariff Protection in Industrial Countries: an Evaluation", *Journal of Political Economy,* 1965.

Basevi, G. "The United States Tariff Structure: estimates of effective rates of protection of United States industries and industrial labor". *Review of Economics and Statistics,* 1966.

Balassa, B et al "The Structure of Protection in Developing Counties", Johns Hopkins University Press, 1971.

Garnaut, Ross, Australia, in Williamson (ed.) The Political Economy of Policy Reform, Institute of International Economics, Washington DC (1994).

Greenaway, David and Chris Milner, "Effective Protection, Policy Appraisal and Trade Policy Reform", *The World Economy,* April 2003

Rattigan, Alf, *Industry Assistance: The Inside Story,* Melbourne University Press, 1986.

12

Melbourne and ANU: Nine Productive Years

This was a remarkable nine-year period for me and my work. But it started with an extremely sad event.

My Father Has a Heart Attack

My father, aged 62, known as *Vati* (German for Daddy), had a heart attack while visiting Adelaide on a selling trip, which he did regularly every six months. The family knew *Vati* had a heart condition, and indeed his lifestyle—smoking and lack of exercise (always using his car)—did not help. Furthermore, cardiac problems were in his family. I know from Uncle Willy's diaries that Willy, like his brother, also had a heart problem. *Vati* was in Adelaide hospital for several months before he passed away.

I know not from my direct knowledge but from what I have been told by a cousin, who was much older than me, that *Vati* (or Rudolf) had been a very ebullient person, a life of the party, in early days, say up to 1932 (when he was 36, and I was 5). Then came a series of sources of worry. First, the family firm Trautner—for which he was partly responsible from

© The Author(s) 2017
W.M. Corden, *Lucky Boy in the Lucky Country*, Palgrave Studies in the History of Economic Thought, DOI 10.1007/978-3-319-65166-8_12

then on—got into financial difficulties. Later came his dismissal as manager (because of Nazi rules) in 1937, and hence his unemployment and the realisation that the family would have to emigrate, and quickly (see Chap. 1). This, indeed, was a desperate crisis but overshadowed by Kristallnacht and followed by a period in Buchenwald. So we ended up, with the help of Aunt Elli, happily, in Australia. But then came his worry about making a living in Australia, and that was not easy, as clearly indicated by his letter to his mother, brother, and sister in Breslau (attached to Chap. 4). I have the impression that he was quite happy in his later period in the Australian Pioneer Corps, and he would not have been promoted to corporal had they had not been satisfied with him. Also, that period solved the problem of bringing in enough money for the family. And then, after the war, from 1946 to 1958 (12 years) life was good, as his business was successful, with my mother working with him, and his ebullience returned. There were weekly poker games with his "mates", a small group of German Jews, some from Breslau.

He was loud and full of stimulating opinions. Both his sons, Gerald and Max, were much more reserved and quiet than he was. But he would have been pleased to meet one of his grandsons, Martin, younger son of Gerald, who had some of his very pleasing characteristics. But Gerald only married a year after *Vati* died, in 1959, so Martin, my father's true successor (also a salesman, but of computers not handbags), never met his grandfather.

I can never forget what I owe to my father, both for ideas and stimulus—especially over the dinner table in Melbourne—and for his efforts to protect his two sons from the impact of the Hitler regime.

It was certainly fortunate that Dorothy and I returned from London to Melbourne in January 1958. Because of the conference of economists at which I presented my "Adelaide" lecture about tariff reform, we were in Adelaide, when *Vati* had his attack. We stayed on during the university vacation period, and then Donald Cochrane, my professor at Melbourne, very helpfully agreed that, because of my father's illness, I could move my base temporarily to the economics department of the University of Adelaide. It was exceptionally convenient that the hospital was right next to the university.

I cannot recall the precise duration, but I know that we were with *Vati* for several months. At first, we stayed in an apartment in North Adelaide and then moved in with my good friend Geoff Harcourt, professor at the University of Adelaide, and his wife, Joan (both recently arrived from Cambridge). Dorothy and I were with my father almost every day and right till the end. I know he greatly appreciated it and especially Dorothy's devotion. And I must add, he had a special eye for attractive women.

My mother kept the business in Melbourne going during this period, but, of course, she came over with Gerald near the end. He died in Adelaide, and there was a funeral with a rabbi. Uncle Willy would have viewed that with approval.

My Teaching Debut

Melbourne provided my debut of teaching, and indeed teaching large classes. For four years, I was first lecturer and then senior lecturer in the university's department of commerce headed by Donald Cochrane. This was a small department. Most of the faculty were in the economics department, headed by Wilfred Prest who had been, of course, "my" Head when I was a student. Donald and I were in charge of the subject "Trade and Development"; Donald taught Development and I taught Trade. The latter included Balance of Payments Theory. In 1961, 146 students sat for the exam in this subject, of which 44 sat for Honours. In all, 111 passed and 19 got Honours. I also taught a separate Honours course on the theory of growth and trade (closely related to my PhD thesis).

A number of my students ended up in senior positions in the public service in Canberra and at least one in the financial world (Charles Goode). Three of the students—Richard Snape, Bob Gregory, and Peter Drake—became professors and outstanding, influential economists as well as my personal friends. Peter became the first Vice Chancellor of the Australian Catholic University. Bob, followed by Richard, pioneered the Australian version of the Dutch Disease theory.

I think that my first teaching year was not very good—too much description and statistics about Australia, which was boring. But by the second year, I had it all worked out. Indeed, my teaching was a great success. I enjoyed it, and many years later, my former students have told me that they loved it besides other compliments that I shall not repeat.

There were three terms and hence three distinct lecture courses every year. The first term was Development, which Donald Cochrane taught, the second term was International Trade (theory), and the third was Balance of Payments (also theory); I taught the last two. The principal and novel feature of Balance of Payments Theory was that I built it around the Swan diagram. This diagram was invented by Trevor Swan of the Australian National University (ANU). It was certainly new and formed an excellent framework. At that time, it had not been published; it was just part of a conference paper. Much later, it was to appear in textbooks, but at that time, only Heinz Arndt teaching in a branch of the University of Melbourne at Canberra and I used it for teaching. We were pioneers. In numerous articles since then, I have used this diagram, and I have taught it in Oxford and later at the School of Advanced International Studies (SAIS) in Washington DC.

I taught trade theory in a special (perhaps novel) way. I felt that many students would not welcome, or even understand, some of the standard expositions of basic trade theory, whether with diagrams or with mathematics. Therefore, I invented the Bob-and-Bert story, which sadly I never published. But it made an impact. Some of my students became secondary-school teachers of economics in Melbourne, and signs of the story apparently have appeared in Victorian students' final examinations. Here I only give an outline, and leave the details to the reader's imagination.

I wanted to explain the basic two-country, two-sector models, originating geometrically with Marshall and then as Heckscher-Ohlin models with two goods and two factors. The actors are Bob and Bert, (i.e. Bob Menzies and Bert Evatt—the latter was the then Leader of the Opposition). The two live on an island and climb for coconuts or fish for oysters, these being their alternative occupations. Factor proportions and intensities (lungs and muscles) come into the picture as do comparative and absolute advantage. There are diminishing returns and potential economies of scale and also benefits of learning. I leave the details to the reader's imagination. All the standard fundamentals of basic trade theory can be explained.

Writing and Lecturing About Tariff Policy

I have already mentioned in Chap. 11, the 1958 Adelaide lecture about tariff-policy reform. It made a big impact, and seeing the extensive newspaper reports gave pleasure to my father in the hospital. Very suddenly, this lecture launched me in Australia as a prominent economist. Much of my time at the University of Melbourne over the next three years or so was spent on writing more papers on that subject, giving talks about it, and responding to reactions. The biggest piece of research was a long paper covering the history, measurement, and other issues entitled "The Tariff" in *The Economics of Australian Industry* edited by Alex Hunter, which I have already mentioned. Alex was a colleague at the University of Melbourne. This paper introduced the concept of *effective protection* in Australia.

More Family

On the family side, around September 1959, we adopted a sweet and very pretty little one-year old girl born in a Victorian country town, whom we named Jane. She had been abandoned and was being looked after by some nurses in the local hospital. Many years later, she and I traced her ancestry. The ancestry of her birth mother, who failed to look after her properly, could be traced to England (Buckinghamshire, to be precise), while nothing was known about her father. Many years later, we got to know her half-brother and his wife. A touching coincidence is that she was born in September 1958, just one day after the death of my father. So I lost a father and found a daughter.

Also, during this early stage of our lives in Melbourne, I got to know Dorothy's family. She was the oldest of five Martin girls and two Martin boys. Her mother, known as Mumma, lived in Melbourne, as did the two brothers and, at that time, three of the four sisters. One sister lived in Sydney. All were married, and there were numerous children. Every Christmas, they would all turn up at Mumma's, and that is where I got to know them. The family background on Mumma's side was British with great-grandparents having emigrated from England and Scotland, and their father's family came from Cornwall (a Celtic part of England). One of their ancestors was descended from John Pasco, the signal officer of HMS *Victory* who hoisted the famous signal ("England Expects Every Man Will Do His Duty") sent by Admiral Nelson, enabling his fleet to win the Battle of Trafalgar.

ANU Canberra 1962–1967: A Very Productive Period

I moved to the economics department of the School of Pacific Studies of the ANU (Australian National University) in January 1962. "Pacific" refers not to peacefulness but to the Pacific and Asia region. Later, the school was renamed the Research School of Pacific and Asian Studies (RSPAS). By 1964, I was a professorial fellow (reader).

The head and founder of the department was Sir John Crawford, a former senior public servant and a very distinguished citizen. I had visited the ANU's other economics department, headed by Trevor Swan, twice during my Melbourne years. At that time, there were a number of outstanding economists at the ANU, notably Trevor Swan, Heinz Arndt, Wilfred Salter, and Ivor Pearce.

There were modest teaching obligations for me because the ANU was primarily research-motivated. This department, right from the beginning, was focused on research on Asian and Pacific area countries. I participated in a programme of research and writing on the Malaysian and Thai economies. It helped that I had recently spent some time in the two countries. My papers dealt with various trade, exchange rate, and balance of payments issues in these countries. But all this gave me plenty of time to write more advanced papers and even booklets with significant international impact. From this point of view, my first period at the ANU was extremely fruitful. It laid the groundwork for the rest of my academic career.

I also had the pleasure of becoming a PhD supervisor (my first at the ANU) for a student who was to make a significant mark in later years. That was Peter Drysdale, who wrote the thesis "Australian-Japanese Trade:

Bilateral Trade in a Many Country World". He went on to become a prominent and influential specialist on Australia-Japan economic relationships, founding and directing the Australia-Japan Research Centre of the ANU. Another notable early PhD student was Peter Drake, who had been (as I mentioned above) my student at Melbourne, and who wrote a very scholarly thesis under the supervision of Heinz Arndt entitled "The Developing Capital Market in Malaya". It was later published as *Financial Development in Malaya and Singapore*. Later he also became the first Vice Chancellor of the Australian Catholic University.

My Publications

In this period, I wrote and published what turned out to become some of my best-known publications. Hence, in a long-run perspective, this was a very fruitful period for me. In addition, I contributed to two books produced in the department about Asian countries, Malaya (as it was then called) and Thailand. It helped that, while I was still at the University of Melbourne, I had visited, and commenced research, on both countries.

Three Papers with International Impact

"The Structure of a Tariff System and the Effective Protective Rate",
    Journal of Political Economy (1966).
"Recent Developments in the Theory of International Trade", Special
    Papers in International Economics, Princeton University (1965).
"The Geometric Representation of Policies to Attain Internal and External
    Balance", *Review of Economic Studies* (1960).

These three papers made an international impact, especially the first, my "star paper", to which I already referred in Chap. 11. The "Recent Developments" paper had a worldwide readership, especially among students. It was originally written for a conference on recent developments in various branches of economics organised at ANU by Heinz Arndt. I was told much later by John Hicks and Bertil Ohlin (both Nobel prize winners) that they liked it very much—possibly because it was written in an old-fashioned (non-mathematical) way. The "Geometric Representation" paper was a substantial improvement on the diagram in the earlier *Economic Journal* paper written at the National Institute, and it also expounded both the Swan and the Salter diagrams for an international readership. For some time, it became a standard reference. These three papers laid the foundations of my international reputation, from which I benefited in later years. Perhaps they were the best that I have ever produced.

Three Australian Books or Papers

Australian Tariff Policy. *Joseph Fisher Lecture* (1967). Reprinted in W M
    Corden, *The Road to Reform: Essays on Australian Economic Policy*
Australian Economic Policy Discussion: A Survey, Melbourne University
    Press.
The Australian Economy: A Volume of Readings. Edited by Heinz Arndt
    and Max Corden.

The Joseph Fisher lecture was my final summary of Australian tariff policy options and recommendations before I left for Oxford. It was comprehensive and "realistic" but, in retrospect, perhaps seems too pragmatic and cautious. The *Australian Policy Discussion* booklet was comprehensive and widely read. Finally, the "Arndt and Corden" book of *Readings* was the initiative of Heinz Arndt and clearly met a need in the market. It published for the first time Trevor Swan's paper with its classic Swan diagram.

In 1964–1965, I went on a one-year international "sabbatical" trip with Dorothy and Jane to Britain and the USA. This included a term at the University of California, Berkeley. In 1966, I was appointed to an Oxford position, as Nuffield Reader in International Economics, a position I took up late in 1967. So, good bye, Canberra and its sunshine!

Bibliography

WM Corden, "The Structure of a Tariff System and the Effective Protective Rate", *Journal of Political Economy*, 1966.

WM Corden, "The Geometric Representation of Policies to Attain Internal and External Balance", *Review of Economic Studies*, 1960.

WM Corden, *Recent Developments in the Theory of International Trade*, Special Papers in International Economics, Princeton University, 1965.

WM Corden, *Australian Economic Policy Discussion: A Survey*, Melbourne University Press, 1968.

WM Corden, with HW Arndt (eds.), *The Australian Economy: A Volume of Readings*, 1963 FW Cheshire,

WM Corden, "Australian Tariff Policy: Options for Reform", First Joseph Fisher Lecture in Commerce at the University of Adelaide, published in *Australian Economic Papers* December 1967.

T W Swan, "Longer-Run Problems of the Balance of Payments", in HW Arndt and WM Corden, *The Australian Economy: A Volume of Readings*, Cheshire, Melbourne, 1963.

TH Silcock and E K Fisk (eds.) *The Political Economy of Independent Malaya: A Case Study in Development*, the Australian National University 1963.

TH Silcock (ed.) *Thailand: Social and Economic Studies in Development*, 1967.

John Hicks, *Value and Capital* (1939).

Bertil Ohlin, *Interregional and International Trade* (1933).

13

Oxford: The Very Best Years

In September 1967, I arrived in Oxford to take up my appointment as Nuffield Reader in International Economics succeeding Sir Roy Harrod, who had just retired. I had also been elected to be a fellow of Nuffield College, where I would have my office (or "rooms"). I had come via Rome, where I had done some consulting work for the Food and Agriculture Organization of the United Nations (FAO) Dorothy and Jane were coming separately by boat.

Why Another Move?

The three of us—Dorothy, Jane, and I—had visited London in 1964, staying in Putney, this having been the first stage of my sabbatical. Not long after we arrived in London Dorothy said, "Why don't we come back here? Why don't you ask Harry if he can find you a job?" That brief remark led to the next turning point in our lives. At the end of 1965, when we were back in Canberra, Harry Johnson wrote "Would you be interested in putting in for the Nuffield Readership in International Economics at Oxford?" He explained that he was an elector, the other six being from Oxford. I hesitated, with various remarks indicating my genuine modesty. But I did apply, and in February 1966, a cable arrived

© The Author(s) 2017
W.M. Corden, *Lucky Boy in the Lucky Country*, Palgrave Studies in the History of Economic Thought, DOI 10.1007/978-3-319-65166-8_13

"Congratulations. The Best Man Won. Harry". That was an offer I could not refuse.

I had been quite settled in Canberra and liked its climate and environment. The ANU provided excellent facilities for productive research, and I had managed to write and get published some internationally successful papers, notably the JPE "Effective Protection" paper and "Recent Developments in the Theory of International Trade". But Dorothy far preferred living in England to living in Australia, whether Melbourne or Canberra. She found England stimulating, and all her life she had been an Anglophile. We also found in Canberra that Jane had learning problems, and we thought that more help might be available in Oxford (as indeed it was). From my point of view, Canberra was peripheral to the world academic community compared with Oxford. Thus, it was indeed an offer that I could not refuse!

The Colleges

I had a lot to learn about Oxford. After all, unlike much of the Oxford faculty, I had not been a student at Oxford.

The most important feature (shared to a lesser extent with Cambridge) was the crucial role of the colleges. They were very independent institutions, each with its own history and, most important, its own financial endowment. Some were old or very old, like Merton College and Balliol, and some were new, like Nuffield and St Antony's. Some were rich, like both Merton and Nuffield, and some were poor, or somewhat poor, like St Peters. Much of Oxford life revolved around the colleges rather than the university as a whole. There were arrangements for wealthy colleges to subsidise poor colleges. Most colleges had primarily undergraduates, with a minority, sometimes a small minority, of postgraduate students. The notable exceptions were Nuffield and St Antony's which were wholly for postgraduates. Also, these two specialised in the social sciences while most other colleges had members (fellows) from many disciplines. A particular feature of the colleges was that they all had dining rooms—sometimes very grand ones—and this encouraged community lunching and dining, even for faculty and students who were not residents. In fact, the colleges were communities, and not just places where one worked, or slept. All this is well known all over the world from numerous books and films. But it does raise the question: What exactly is the role of the university? Basically it has its own research funding and management, and there is a division of labour in respect to teaching between the colleges (providing tutorials for undergraduates) and the university (providing senior staff, lectures, seminars, and examinations).

The arrangements are actually more complicated than this, but after a while, I realised that it was all very familiar. It reminded me of the Australian federation and the six states with their separate histories and great sense of independence, with the conflicts between the Commonwealth and the states and the debates about the separation of power and of functions, and also the allocation of centrally collected funds by taxation. Oxford was just a loose federation.

My Three Duties and My Two Sources of Income

I was responsible for graduate teaching in the subfield of International Economics for the whole university. Thus, my responsibilities were not limited to students from Nuffield College. In fact, all my three activities were carried on physically in Nuffield College, but that was just a convenience. All three duties were designed for postgraduate students based in any college, though undergraduates could come, and sometimes did come, to my lectures.

The duties were (1) a weekly lecture, (2) a weekly seminar, and (3) individual supervision of students. The allocation of supervisors was done by a university committee. I took these duties very seriously and gave them priority over any other activities, notably research and writing.

My income came primarily from the university because the readership was a university appointment. All professors and most readers came under this category. But all fellows of Nuffield College who were university appointments (and thus not ordinary fellows) received a modest supplement from the college. This reflected the fact that Nuffield was basically a rich college, and most other colleges probably did not pay such supplements to their university-appointed fellows.

My seminar was carefully organised. (This was the German in me.) The weekly programme would be available at the beginning of each term. Each week, either a student or a visitor presented a paper. The student was required to have his or her paper ready in advance by a precise date, and I would usually check it to ensure the quality. A highlight would be that every year Harry Johnson would come from the LSE (where he had moved, from Manchester) and give a talk, followed by sherry for the students (and whisky for Harry) in my room. I would have substantial reading lists in advance for each seminar topic. (Actually, I am not sure now whether Harry would give a paper or a student would do so. The same question arises with respect to other visitors.)

The Nuffield College Experience

The whole Oxford experience was terrific, but really outstanding was being a fellow of Nuffield. Possibly the same could be said about other colleges, but here I write only about my own experience. It was like becoming a member of a family—a prosperous family with a high average IQ and education, a variety of personalities, but, above all, a sense of identity and "fellowship". Perhaps this recollection is exaggerated, even romantic. I am now 89 years old, and I was 40 when I came to Nuffield and 49 when I left. No doubt things have changed, and my memory may not be accurate. But histories of Nuffield will give more detailed facts. Here I should just note that the college started post-war on the basis of generous endowments from Lord Nuffield. One of these endowments was Nuffield Place, which was once Lord Nuffield's home (located in the village of Nuffield, near Henley) and in which we could gather in various community activities, with family, in summer.

There were regular meetings during term time (there were three terms a year), when all the Fellows would meet, with the warden in the chair, to discuss all aspects of college business, including selection of students. Nuffield had enough funds to pay for its students, and hence select them. The warden was not a dictator but a first among equals and did not always get his way. But warden Chester was utterly devoted to the interests of the college. Such meetings, combined with lunching together and dining at least every Friday evening during term time, and also some other times, meant that a sense of collegiality was developed. Perhaps it was the same in other colleges?

Some Nuffield Colleagues

Even though it is 40–49 years ago, I have a recollection of many of my Nuffield colleagues. Here, let me just mention a few. Maurice Scott, formerly a fellow of Christ Church, was basically an applied economist, working on the UK economy and international aspects. He was the fellow closest to me both personally and in areas of interest. He was, above all, a very straightforward, honourable person, who always said, though politely, what he thought and with great common sense. He was also, unlike me, a good college man, having been a bursar (looking after investments) for many years after I left. It was common for students of Nuffield who specialised in the areas of international or development economics to be jointly supervised by him and me. I represented the university and he the college. His last work, before I left, was a big study, both theoretical and statistical, on economic growth.

John Flemming was much younger than I was, and quite brilliant, a master of all difficult theory issues, and also interested in the British economy. He was an incredibly fast and subtle thinker and speaker, with plenty of common sense. I always felt he was far smarter than I was but, for some reason, I managed to write and publish far more. For some time after I left, he was an economist with the Bank of England and then chief economist of the newly created European Bank for Reconstruction and Development. Tragically he died at age 60 from prostate cancer and by then he had become warden of Wadham College.

What both Maurice and John had in common was that they had been bursars (for investment) and generally were active in college management. Another economist in the College was Aubrey Silberston, his field having been industry economics. Like the above two he was very applied, concerned with the British economy, but not as theoretical as John or me.

All four of us, but particularly John and I, talked a lot with students in the junior common room during morning or afternoon tea and other occasions. I think this was a significant contribution to college life and was much appreciated by the students.

But there were many other fellows with whom I was friendly. Frances Seton specialised on the economy of the Soviet Union and was less communicative than the others I have mentioned. He was born in Vienna and much older than we were. He was a very cultivated, civilised person. Max Hartwell was an Australian (with a marked Australian accent and style), who was a notable person in economic history, and, had written important articles suggesting that the standard of living of the English working class had actually improved during the industrial revolution. I understand that this was contrary to the views of some well-known Marxists historians. He loved being provocative, or at least outspoken. Thus, he was rather different from me even though we both had our names and country in common; hence (to quote David Butler), we were *maxi Max* and *mini Max*, I being the latter. Max Hartwell told me that he polished his Australian accent in front of the mirror every morning. Yet he had been in Oxford since 1956! Incidentally, he was the keeper of the Nuffield wine cellar.

In addition to economists, Nuffield had both sociologists and political studies (or political science) people. I found these colleagues very interesting. The latter often brought distinguished political figures to college dinners as guests. We have had the outstanding sociologist, and just an outstanding human being, Chelly Halsey, who had many widely read books to his credit. Another outstanding figure was David Butler, famous both for his election studies and for his political contacts which led to interesting visitors to Nuffield.

Three Famous Economists

Of the following three economists, John Hicks was a former fellow of Nuffield, and while I was in Oxford held the most senior Oxford chair, namely the Drummond professorship based at All Souls College (from which he retired while I was there). Ian Little was a Nuffield colleague for almost the whole time I was there, and Jim Mirrlees came from Cambridge to Oxford and Nuffield College as Edgeworth professor in 1969.

One could write a great deal about these three major figures, and here I just focus on my connection with them.

John Hicks (1904–1989)

He is so famous I do not need to list all the reasons for that, except that he was the first Englishman to get the Nobel Prize for economics (which he shared with the American Kenneth Arrow). His fame is based on highly influential writings—especially *Value and Capital*—all produced in the thirties.

I first met John Hicks and his wife, Ursula (a prominent applied economist in her own right), when they visited the ANU in 1966. At that point, I had already been appointed to the Nuffield readership but was not due to actually take it up until late 1967. In fact, at first, I was unduly shy, awed by the great man. In retrospect, that seems silly. John was delighted to give me lots of gossip and advice about Nuffield individuals. At the same time, Ursula and Dorothy bonded owing to a common interest in gardening.

When we were settling in Oxford, they went out of their way to welcome us. There is a grand occasion—the *Encaenia*—which is the annual ceremony of the honorary degree awards; it is followed by a grand lunch for the distinguished visitors who get the honorary degrees, and only a select number of Oxford people were invited. The lunch took place at All Souls College, and Dorothy and I were guests of John and Ursula. We were impressed!

Subsequently they invited us several times to their house—a historic house in Blockley, a charming village in the Cotswolds. I feel we got to know them both very well, and it was my mistake not to have taken the opportunity to know more about their past. They would not have felt my questions to be intrusive. I am sure now that they would actually have welcomed them. I could have written much more here about how John came to write his various famous prewar papers and what impressions he had of his notable LSE colleagues. He did tell me that he was (more recently) on a committee jointly with Nicholas Kaldor (and others) to do with taxation and found Kaldor difficult to deal with.

I now know that he had a favourable view of me, and especially of my "Recent Developments in the Theory of International Trade" (written at ANU), and that caused him to support my appointment to the Nuffield readership. He had actually been on the committee that appointed me.

There is an extended review of John Hicks' life and work in *Biographical Memoirs of Fellows of the British Academy XII* (2013), pp. 215–231 by John Creedy. This contains the following footnote:

> The present writer's experience of Hicks in discussion is largely from the magnificent graduate seminars on welfare economics held in Nuffield College, which were led by Max Corden. In response to a question, Hicks would take several different paths in turn, each time stopping mid-way with a long silence, until producing his final eloquent preferred response.

Ian Little

He was the outstanding economist at Nuffield and Oxford (after Hicks) when I arrived there. His fame was really based on a classic book, *A Critique of Welfare Economics*. It was a brilliant piece of critical theory, very profound, and it immediately made his reputation. He wrote it while he was a student. It was undoubtedly negative. But he has himself admitted that, in spite of his negativity about the intellectual foundations of welfare economics as it had then developed, his later work was actually applied welfare economics. Later he wrote that "rough theory, or good common sense is, in practice what we require". I agree with that. Indeed, common sense and intellectual honesty have been his trademark.

Ian was the initiator and team leader *of Industry and Trade in Some Developing Countries,* written jointly with Tibor Scitovsky and Maurice Scott (hence LSS for short), which had just been completed when I came to Oxford. This project has been very influential in affecting development policy. Based on detailed studies of individual countries, they concluded that import-replacement policies had failed. It was the success of this project that led Ian to propose to the World Bank a comparative multi-country project, Macroeconomic Experience of Developing Countries, a big and demanding project in which I (and others) participated.

I don't think that our project was as successful as LSS, at least by the criteria of citations and policy impact. The reason is that we did not oppose a prevalent conventional wisdom and so start an intellectual revolution. I have more to say about it in Chap. 16.

Personally, Ian could be rather reserved and sometimes I worried, as his colleague in this project: What was he thinking? I, Max, am rather inclined to be loquacious. Perhaps on that matter, on the average, Ian and I together were just average. He died in 2012.

Jim Mirrlees

He came to Nuffield in 1969 as Edgeworth Professor of Economics. Previously he had been at Cambridge. He and I shared a secretary, and I saw a lot of him. On the whole, I did not understand what he was saying and what he was working on. It turned out that during this period, when he was my close colleague, he did the outstanding work for which he later shared (with William Vickrey) the Nobel Prize. This was awarded "for their fundamental contribution to the economic theory of incentives under asymmetric information". Among other things, he demonstrated the principles of "moral hazard" and of "optimal income taxation". I am afraid that my lack of understanding says something unfavourable about me. He was a nice, polite person, who was pushing hard to bring more mathematics into the Oxford B Phil (now M Phil) education. I seem to recall that this encountered opposition from outside Nuffield.

My Two Closest Colleagues: Peter Oppenheimer and Vijay Joshi

In Nuffield, my closest colleague was Maurice Scott. He was involved with supervision of writers of graduate theses in trade and development, but not with teaching. With respect to the weekly seminar in international economics and the lectures, my two closest colleagues were based in other colleges. They were Peter Oppenheimer, at Christ Church College and Vijay Joshi at Merton College. They attended the weekly seminar with me and contributed to the discussion. They also lectured on trade theory (Vijay) and international monetary theory (Peter). In the area of international macroeconomics, I felt that Peter knew a lot more than I did. He lectured on it, and he helped me understand some issues. When I returned to Oxford from giving the Abbott lectures in Chicago in 1976, I started writing it up in my book entitled *Inflation, Exchange Rates and the World Economy*. This was a fairly new field for me, and I had a lot to learn. To quote from the Introduction: "I have been much influenced by lengthy discussions while striding along the banks of the Isis with my Oxford colleague Peter Oppenheimer, and his thoughtful comments at a later stage gave me many days work of revising the manuscript". That says it all. (The Isis is the name of the Thames in Oxford). Also, we published a joint paper "Economic Issues for the Oil Importing Countries" in a book edited by Tad Rybczynski, *The Economics of the Oil Crisis* (1976).

With Vijay, I have had continuous discussions on trade theory. See the Acknowledgements to *Trade Policy and Economic Welfare*. His main publications until recently have been two books on India jointly with Ian Little: *India: Macroeconomics and Political Economy 1964–1991* and *India's Economic Reforms 1991–2001*. But his most recent book is his magnum opus, *India's Long Road: The Search for Prosperity* (2016). I believe that this is likely to make an enormous impact.

The Students

One of the great attractions of Oxford, and a small number of other, similar universities, is the high quality of so many of the students. A lot of them were stimulating talkers, but their quality only became clear to me later, when they were very successful in various careers. Many came to the International Economics seminar, and a smaller number were my personally supervised students. Some, notably but not only John Martin and Christopher Smallwood, have become close personal friends over 40 years. Peng Teh was already a good friend when he came to Oxford. I cannot claim credit for their success in later life, but I can immodestly bathe in reflected glory. But modesty prevents me from citing the various honours they have received. I am sure I have left out some I should have included, but here I list them alphabetically by surnames. It was a pleasure to teach and interact with them, and I am impressed with their achievements. This was one of the great pleasures of spending nine years in Oxford.

Roger Bootle, Paul Collier, John Creedy, John Llewellyn, John Martin, Peter Neary, Frances Ruane, Peter Sinclair, Christopher Smallwood, Nicholas Stern, Peng Teh, Martin Wolf.

Books and Articles

Effective Protection and the Theory of Protection

My JPE "Effective Protection" article was published in 1966, just before I arrived in Oxford. It then led to many people writing articles about it, or writing directly to me. It was quite a literature that developed. In my first three years in Oxford, all this took up much of my time. Frequently two critical points were made, namely (1) that the *effective rate* was a partial equilibrium concept and did not allow for general equilibrium, and (2) that the so-called substitution problem was fatal to the concept. This led me to write and publish two articles, namely

"Effective Protective Rates in the General Equilibrium Model: A Geometric Note", *Oxford Economic Papers*, July 1969

"The Substitution Problem in the Theory of Effective Protection" *Journal of International Economics*, February 1971 (this was in the first issue of a new journal).

I also had the following thought. Traditionally, the theory of protection as presented in textbooks and elsewhere had taken two forms: first the *partial equilibrium approach*, where one just analysed protection of one product, with no protection or intervention elsewhere, and second, the *two-good (exportables and importables) general equilibrium approach* as pioneered diagrammatically by Alfred Marshall. But it is the in-between *multigood general equilibrium* case that is closer to the real world, and needed to be developed.

I then embarked on writing a book of positive economics that would make everything clear and spell out many complications, and with a multigood emphasis. It would replace and go beyond my 1966 effective protection article. This book was *The Theory of Protection* (1971), my first book written in Oxford. It included the two articles listed above as chapters. In view of all the difficulties and complications in this field, it also had a pragmatic conclusion. I tried to take care of all the issues involved in a realistic and useful body of theory, where effective protection is only one part of the story. It also has an Appendix on the history of the effective-protection idea, and a bibliography of about 70 items.

The reviews were generally very favourable, but one of them ends: "Nevertheless, the lengthy development of certain issues may be a bit trying for the impatient reader". I agree! *The Economist* review was highly favourable: "his treatment, besides containing new elements, is an altogether admirable piece of exposition. ... He has none of the exhibitionism which makes the writing of some theorists difficult to follow".

Inevitably this book was not easy-reading and certainly not destined to be a bestseller. It was a rather dense book for serious students, and as such I believe it met a need, and was well-received.

Trade Policy and Economic Welfare

Having finished *The Theory of Protection*, I moved to a book that would comprehensibly expound and analyse the *normative* theory of trade policy, with an emphasis on policy relevance. This was a big venture. This book would incorporate eight articles that I had earlier published in this area, and much else. *Trade Policy and Economic Welfare* (1974), was to some extent inspired by Meade's *Trade and Welfare*, and has been my most ambitious enterprise.

I think it is much easier to read than my first book: there are lots of subheadings, diagrams, and simple explanations, with very little mathematics. Both citations and sales suggest this book is the one by which I might be remembered. In 1997, it went into a second edition, which had four new chapters and replaced three existing Chaps. (6, 13, and 14). One particular concept is new and has attracted much interest and citations. That is the *conservative social welfare function*. I think that this concept helps to explain now (2016) the revival of protectionism in the USA, and possibly elsewhere.

The reviews were generally very favourable, but Anne Krueger makes a good point: "Çorden has bent over backward to give every conceivable argument for intervention a fair hearing", and Harry Johnson, while impressed by the organisation around a theme (best, second-best, etc.), thinks I have overdone the possible second-best and worse arguments for intervention (distinguish scholarly responsibility from "academic priggishness"). Ivor Pearce criticises the implicit assumption that governments can get it right, are detached, and so on. In fact, all the criticisms are along the same lines, with which I sympathise.

A Survey of Customs Union Theory

For a complete review of trade and protection theory, one cannot ignore customs union theory. So I proceeded to survey this body of theory, beginning with the writings of Jacob Viner, James Meade, and Richard Lipsey. This turned out to be a very elaborate body of literature, with great scope for taxonomy. When I finished it, I decided not to publish it separately because it did not seem to be sufficiently original or interesting. But I did pick out two cases where there had been gaps in the literature and where I had something to add. This then led to the following two articles. The first of these has made considerable impact. It really filled an important gap and was relevant for an analysis of the effects of the new European Union. Therefore, it has been much cited and reprinted.

"Economies of Scale and Customs Union Theory", *Journal of Political Economy*, May/June 1972.
"Customs Union Theory and the Non-Uniformity of Tariffs", *Journal of International Economics,* February 1976.

Many years later, I published this whole customs union survey as part of a large and comprehensive survey of the normative theory of international trade. See "Customs Union Theory", in *Handbook of International Economics Volume 1,* edited by Ronald W. Jones and Peter Kenen, North Holland (1984d), pp. 112–124.

The Big Switch: To International Macroeconomics

The Theory of Protection and *Trade Policy and Economic Welfare* plus the customs union survey completed my work on protection and trade policy. This, I thought, was more than enough. I did not want to spend my whole life on one branch of economics. There is so much interesting happening, or likely to happen, in the world. So I made the Big Switch.

The first step was my response to an invitation to give the Graham lecture in Princeton. European Monetary Union was much under discussion, so I chose *monetary integration* as my topic. As usual, I would try and sort out the fundamental issues.

The second step was to accept an invitation to give the three Abbott lectures at the Graduate School of Business of the University of Chicago, and here I chose to deal with a number of topics, notably "inflation and exchange rates" and "the international adjustment to the oil price rise". In these lectures, I would also deal with some basic theoretical issues. All this reflected my inclination to choose my research topics with the aim of sorting out current real-world issues. It is this inclination that originally brought me to the theory of protection, when I looked at Australian policy issues. Later on (near the end of my Oxford period), the same attitude would lead me to study closely the reasons for the sharp appreciation of the pound sterling under Mrs Thatcher's government at a time of Britain's North Sea oil boom, and thus brought me to Dutch Disease theory (on which see Chap. 14).

Monetary Integration

Princeton University April 1972. *Essays in International Finance No 93*

In 2016, 46 years after its publication, I am reading this essay in the light of the recent Eurozone crisis.

My Judgement Now The essay has two faults: (1) it brings in too many (probably unimportant) considerations; it is too much a literature survey. (2) It fails to ask the crucial question: Will monetary union increase the probability of asymmetric shocks?

Its virtue is that it makes clearly the main point, also made in other of my writings, that the need for, and effectiveness of, each country making real exchange rate adjustment hinges on the downward flexibility of nominal wages (in response to unemployment) and the flexibility of real wages (in response to devaluation). That is clearly expounded on pp. 11–12 of the essay.

Recent Crisis Experience I focus on Greece, Spain, and Ireland here. They suffered asymmetric shocks because of excess borrowing by their private sectors and also (in the case of Greece) by the public sector. Hence, they had crises and needed to cut spending to pay off debts, and this caused austerity. That could have been avoided if the real exchange rate (and real wages) had fallen enough, bringing about the necessary improvement of competitiveness. But this did not happen!

(a) **Asymmetric shocks**: The monetary union actually caused or encouraged such shocks. There had been too much lending by international capital to private sectors in all three countries, and to the government in Greece, because of a false sense of security. That sense of security was created by having a monetary union. If the three countries had their own monetary policies, with good management, the central banks would have raised interest rates to discourage excess borrowing. But the interest rate they faced was too low (to suit Germany).

(b) **The adjustment problem**: Surely nominal wages were not sufficiently flexible downwards, otherwise unemployment would have been avoided. The devotees to free markets (including Harry Johnson) were wrong in assuming such flexibility. Nominal wages were *somewhat* flexible but not enough. That is evident. But could devaluation have helped or was there real wage rigidity? In the rigidity case, nominal wage increases would have offset the beneficial effects of devaluation. That has not been tested. I think there probably would have been some degree of flexibility, that is devaluations would have been partially *real*, and thus partially effective. One has to look at evidence from other episodes and countries.

Conclusion Availability of their own exchange rate would have eased (but not solved) the problem. But perhaps, without the union there might not have been a problem because they would not have been able to borrow so readily.

Inflation, Exchange Rates and the World Economy: Lectures on International Monetary Economics (1977)

These are the Abbott lectures and are published by the OUP and University of Chicago Press. This was my third book written and published in Oxford. It turned out to be very popular because it dealt with current issues.

It covered the following four broad topics:

Balance of Payments Theory, old and new; inflation and exchange rates; international adjustment to the oil-price rise; and monetary integration in Europe.

There were many reviews (I have a list of 19), and they were very favourable. This book was widely found stimulating. I value especially the careful and extremely favourable review by Gottfried Haberler (in *The Journal of Money, Credit and Banking*). Perhaps this has been my best-written, and possibly most popular, book.

An Article in the Development Economics Area

During the Oxford period, I published a number of articles mentioned above and also some others, sometimes incorporated eventually in the two main books. And there were others, not listed here. But I must make special mention of the following article written jointly with an old friend, Ronald Findlay of Columbia University:

"Urban Unemployment, International Capital Mobility and Development Policy", *Economica*, February 1975.

Our article is a geometric exposition in a simple way of the Harris-Todaro urban unemployment model. This model is a classic analysis by Professors Harris and Todaro, and based on their Kenyan experience, of the causes of specifically urban unemployment (as distinct from overall unemployment) in developing countries. Our article, with its neat two-sector diagrams, has become a standard reference in development economics, always mentioned in development textbooks, and heavily cited. It was, indeed, an unexpected success. Ron and I had been working on this topic independently. We met when I visited Columbia University (while based in Princeton), and we decided there to combine when we discovered we had both worked on this model, but with different diagrams. The result has become for me (and perhaps Ron) one of our most cited articles.

How I Spent My Time

While in Oxford, I gave absolute priority to my teaching duties and then my writing—and hence wrote three books. Perhaps I should (and did) feel guilty, but I avoided college and university duties. I was asked to chair a university committee concerned with graduate students, but declined it, and might have done more in college (domestic bursar?) But I did make a college contribution by talking a lot with students, more than some fellows, thus being very accessible. Perhaps that was my main contribution. I avoided all public engagements. One did not find me on the morning train to Whitehall. I had been more publicly active in Australia.

With regard to public affairs, the exception was a paper written jointly with Ian Little and Maurice Scott about possible import controls in the UK—in opposition to a Cambridge proposal. My contribution was the phrase "Import controls breed corruption like beetles in a dung heap"—that made headlines, since the debate became prominent in the press. Naturally an Oxford versus Cambridge "battle" had some appeal to the press.

I also spent much time refereeing articles for journals. There were various journals, but a high proportion of my work consisted of refereeing for the *Oxford Economic Papers*. In some cases, I wrote very full reports. I often made suggestions for improvement and tried to avoid being too negative. I also responded to many letters from all over the world, the main topic being effective protection.

Visits, Conferences During My Oxford Years

I did a lot of travelling during my nine years in Oxford. Here is a condensed list.

UK Treasury, Queens University, Ontario (one week), World Bank (three weeks), Brookings (European Monetary Integration), Mannheim (monetary integration), Bank of England (host: Leslie Dicks-Mireaux), Dublin, Civil Service College, *Bicentenary of The Wealth of Nations*, Glasgow April 1976 (major event, commented in a paper by Marcus Fleming, met F. A. von Hayek, J J Polak), Aberystwyth, Cambridge, Geneva. In addition, I visited Melbourne three times, based once in each of the three Universities (Melbourne, Monash, and La Trobe).

Some General Thoughts About Coming to Oxford

Perhaps these were the best, most memorable, nine years of our lives. The first year we lived in Blandford Avenue, North Oxford, in the house of the Maurice Scott family (who was working in Paris for the OECD). After that, we purchased a house on Harcourt Hill, a wonderful location, with great views. First Jane went to North Hinksey Primary School, and then (for secondary school) to a Quaker boarding school near Chipping Norton. We usually picked her up and brought her home every weekend, or we picked her up and went somewhere, like Chipping Norton. She always had learning problems and also difficult relationships with other children. She was nine when we arrived and 18 when we left. We (Dorothy) acquired a dog, a Llasa Apso. Very important!

We had two longer visits from Dorothy's mother (Mumma) and one from my mother (*Mutti*). Dorothy's sister, Ruth, stayed with us for long periods. She was very helpful when we entertained, and also company for Dorothy. Also, my brother and family visited, staying in the house of a neighbour, when she was on holiday or away. On weekends, we often had a visit from my cousin Henni from London. She and Jane were very good friends. About halfway through our nine-year period, Dorothy took a course in librarianship, and for two to three years towards the end, she was assistant librarian at Jesus College (came home as Mrs Jesus). The highlights of our Oxford period were numerous visits to Cotswold villages, and sometimes further. We loved Burford. Also, there were many visits to Stratford, usually overnight, to see one play, or even two. And we had many visitors from Australia. We usually took them for trips to Cotswold villages.

We entertained colleagues very little at home (since the college filled that role), but students a lot. Here Ruth was very helpful. Students have told me many years later how much they appreciated these occasions. Dorothy was a great hostess.

On one occasion, I had arranged for James Meade to visit Oxford, primarily for dining in college, but I also had him at home for an evening, and I invited a group of students to meet him. Many years later, I went to a conference in London in honour of the centenary of James Meade's birth (1907). Also present was Sir Nicholas (now Lord) Stern, who was just Nick Stern when he was a student. I had invited Nick and some others. On that centenary occasion, he mentioned that he first met James Meade at our home, how much he appreciated that and now that he was a professor at the LSE he did the same for his students. I was naturally pleased to hear this. Unfortunately, Dorothy (who had Alzheimer's by 2007) could not benefit from this knowledge.

One of the highlights of our Oxford years were the many visitors, both academic and personal, that we enjoyed—usually in combination with Cotswold travelling. Oxford is so well located, and so attractive in itself, that everybody loved to come. Some academic friends stayed for long periods—like Ronald Findlay and Carlos Diaz-Alejandro, or Henryk Kierzkowski, and some I got know for the first time—Bob Solow and Charles Kindleberger—who became friends, and indeed many others.

Why Did We Leave?

Our leaving Oxford to return to Australia (Canberra) was a great surprise to my Nuffield colleagues and perhaps others. We did not leave out of any dissatisfaction with Oxford. If money were an issue I could have gone to USA every summer (in my case, Chicago) for a limited period, and that is what many British academics, especially Oxford people, did to supplement their incomes. And, as must be clear from what I have written, we loved Oxford, and I also loved my job and had no desire for promotion—that is becoming a professor. No, there were two factors: firstly, Dorothy was very keen to be closer to her mother as she got older, as we would be if we returned to Canberra, and, most important, we felt that Jane would be better off—more comfortable and adjusted—in Australia. Fortunately, my brother, Gerald, lived in Melbourne, so frequent visits to Melbourne from Oxford seemed to fulfil my need or obligation to be with my mother (who was in an aged home then). As she grew older though, I did feel a little guilty on this matter. But I think that Jane was the main concern.

Just one thing was clearly better in Canberra than in Oxford, but it was not a reason to leave. And that was the weather! But I do remember my impression of Canberra when we returned: that utterly blue sky! I think I did write back: "this is like living in Majorca (or was it Minorca?) with a university!"

Bibliography

WM Corden, *The Theory of Protection*, Clarendon Press, Oxford 1971.

WM Corden, *Trade Policy and Economic Welfare*, Clarendon Press, Oxford 1974.

WM Corden, *Inflation, Exchange Rates, and the World Economy: Lectures on International Monetary Economics*, Clarendon Press, Oxford, 1977.

WM Corden, *Monetary Integration*, Essays in International Finance, International Finance Section, Princeton University, April 1972.

WM Corden with Ronald Findlay, "Urban Unemployment, Intersectoral Capital Mobility and Development", *Economica* vol 42 1975.

AH Halsey, *No Discouragement: An Autobiography*, Macmillan Press, 1996.

John Hicks, *Value and Capital*, 1939.

Ian Little, *A Critique of Welfare Economics*, 1950.

Ian Little, with R. Scitovsky and MFG Scott (LSS), *Industry and Trade in Some Developing Countries*, Oxford University Press 1970.

Ian Little, with R Cooper, WM Corden and S Rajapatirana, *Boom, Crisis, and Adjustment: The Macroeconomic Experience of Developing Countries*, Oxford University Press for the World Bank, 1993.

Vijay Joshi, *India's Long Road: The Search for Prosperity*, Oxford University Press, 2016.

Peter Oppenheimer, with WM Corden, "Economic Issues for the Oil Importing Countries" in T. Rybczynski (ed.) *The Economics of the Oil Crisis*, 1976.

John Creedy, "John Hicks", *Biographical Memoirs of Fellows of the British Academy*, 2013.

14

ANU: Dutch Disease and Other Issues

On the family side, living in Canberra, we were able to see much more of our mothers in Melbourne. This, of course, was a major reason why we had come back to Australia. We bought a house in the Canberra suburb of Forrest—an ideal location. We enjoyed lots more sunshine, but that was not a reason for coming back but rather a bonus. We set up Jane in a very nice apartment with a fine view, in the suburb of Campbell. Then she met her fate, namely she met John Shallis (married and with children). Eventually, in 1981, they married, and we arranged the wedding in Melbourne, jointly with the 80th birthday of my mother. Both our families (the Martins and the Cordens) were present. Dorothy's brother was the best man. Our beloved Aunt Elli (having moved from England to Melbourne when her husband died) was also present.

Department Head at the ANU

For a period of about six years, I was head of the Department of Economics at ANU in which I was based. It was part of the Research School of Pacific and Asian Studies. Some explanation, and commentary on the issues involved, is needed.

© The Author(s) 2017
W.M. Corden, *Lucky Boy in the Lucky Country*, Palgrave Studies in the History of Economic Thought, DOI 10.1007/978-3-319-65166-8_14

I succeeded Heinz Arndt, who was due to retire in 1980. To put it briefly, I seemed to be the most suitable person available at that time even though I was rather reluctant. I continued to write articles on a variety of topics, and not primarily on regional (Asia and Pacific) area studies, as did about half the other researchers in the department at that time. I managed also to do some successful recruitment of staff (in the field of development or international economics), but I was able to do all this because there was no systematic large-class teaching required. It was research (and graduate education) only—and that requires some remarks about the ANU.

The ANU was established after the war (1946) by the federal government as an elite institution with a responsibility for research and graduate education. As the population of the Australian Capital Territory (ACT) grew, there was a need for undergraduate education, and that was met by the University of Melbourne establishing a branch in Canberra, quite distinct from the ANU. Much later (in 1960), the Research Schools—of which the Research School of Pacific and Asian Studies (RSPAS) was one—were combined with the original University of Melbourne teaching school, and the combination was also named Australian National University (ANU). But, of course, the Research Schools in various fields continued with their research and graduate education.

I joined the economics department within the RSPAS, twice, first after Melbourne from 1962 to 1967, and now, after Oxford, from 1977 to 1986. I was a perfect match for the research function, and the ANU was a perfect match for me.

The Indonesia Project

In the nine years that I was in Oxford, Heinz Arndt, as head of the ANU (RSPAS) economics department (successor to Sir John Crawford), had established, managed, and actively participated in the Indonesia project within the department. This was a project which involved close study of the Indonesian economy and also bringing scholars and students from Indonesia to the ANU. This was Heinz's principal and highly successful innovation. By September 2016, this project had lasted 50 years. Since 1980, it has been supported financially by the Australian government.

In October 2016, University of Melbourne hosted a visit and an outstanding lecture from an ANU PhD graduate, currently Professor of Economics at the University of Indonesia, and recent Finance Minister of Indonesia, Dr Chatib Basri. He was a "product" of this project. Indonesia is Australia's major neighbour, a nation of 250 million people, so such a project is surely appropriate. The project has published not only The *Bulletin of Indonesian Economic Studies*, which has regularly contained surveys of the Indonesian economy (which Heinz often used to write) but also articles on many specialised topics. The training of young Indonesian PhD economists has been a particularly useful legacy of the project. There have sometimes been as many as ten Indonesian PhD students at the department at any one time. In the Indonesian Yudhoyono cabinet, the vice president (Boediono) had a Monash graduate degree, but had been mentored in the department, and then became a junior member of staff. The finance minister, the trade minister, and the foreign minister were all ANU graduates. Also, crucial among strong supporters, and from time to time staff members, have been prominent Indonesian public intellectuals like Thee Kian Wee and Hadi Soesastro.

When I returned from Oxford, Heinz was concerned about the future prospects of his "baby" (the Indonesia project) when he retired. He hoped that I would work on, or write about Indonesia, perhaps writing a survey. A fair request! Somehow, he formed the impression that, if I became head of the department, I might abolish the project. Actually, I had no such thought. Indeed, I had not thought about it, whether positive or negative. I cannot remember what I did say, but it must have been unwise. But, sadly, it did affect our long-standing relationship. The moral which I have drawn (for the benefit of all younger people) is: speech is silver, but silence is golden. The latter is safer!

Anyway, the Indonesia project still exists. How did this happen? When Heinz retired in 1980, several of his students took over in turn: first Peter McCawley, then, for 12 years, from 1986 to 1998 Hal Hill, then Chris Manning, and in 2011 the first Indonesian head, Budy Resosudarmo. Hal Hill produced an outstanding book, a major product of the project, *The Indonesian Economy* (1996 first edition), which, I can recall, was referred to in Washington DC, when I was there during the Asian Crisis (1997–1999). Above all, now in 2017, the project still exists, the flagship of the department.

My Publications on Asian Topics

The focus of most members of the department was, and is, on economic development and Asia area studies, not either theory or Australian policy. But in this period, I did have a number of publications that fitted into the department's main Asia field, in particular *Macroeconomic Targets and Instruments for a Small Open Economy* (1984) written explicitly for the Singapore case while I was in Singapore, *The Petroleum Boom and Exchange Rate Policy in Indonesia: A Theoretical Analysis,* (1981), written jointly with Peter Warr and published in Indonesia and finally, *Reflections on Japan and the World Economy* (1983), a paper written for the Group of Thirty, and published in Japan.

Wages and Unemployment in Australia

In 1978, shortly after I returned to the ANU from Oxford, I was made president of the Economic Society of Australia. I gave the presidential address on the hot subject of "Wages and Unemployment in Australia". This (and other talks) brought me quite deep into current Australian debates. I doubt that I had the same impact as I had in 1958–1967 with regard to Australian protection policy, but it was somewhat comparable.

The background is that Australia had two wages explosions: one in 1974–1975 under the Whitlam government and the other in 1981–1982 under the Fraser government caused, in part, by a resources boom that was expected but did not actually happen. A relevant fact is that Australia had a centralised system of wage determination. The other basic fact is that over this period (from 1974), unemployment increased markedly. It was the view of the secretary of the Australian Treasury, and of some Australian economists, notably Richard Snape, that the wage increases caused the excessive unemployment, and that, therefore, an improvement in the employment situation required wage restraint of some kind. This put a focus on the wage determination process. It really reflected a "neo-classical" way of thinking. I shared this view and explored it in some depth in various talks and writings, notably my 1979 presidential address.

But there was an alternative and widely held view: unemployment could and should be reduced by expansionary Keynesian fiscal or mone-tary policies. This appeared to be orthodox Keynesianism. It assumed implicitly that a rise in prices caused by such policies would be allowed by trade unions to reduce real wages and not be followed by higher nomi-nal wages in an indexation process. Yet indexation, through the central-ised wage determination process, had been built into the Australian system. Indeed, it was the source of the problem.

A Tax-Wage Bargain?

The Melbourne Institute of Economic and Social Research made the practical recommendation that taxes should be reduced, so that wages pressure would also be reduced, since the unions would aim to maintain real *after-tax* wages, and either the subsequent reduction in nominal wages or the increased demand would reduce unemployment. This was the policy of a "tax-wage bargain". Peter Dixon (from Monash University) and I examined this proposal in depth making use of Dixon's general equilibrium model. We published this in *The Economic Record* as "A Tax Wage Bargain: Is a Free Lunch Possible?" (1980).

To some extent, the Labor Hawke government's "Accord" of 1983 was a form of income policy that succeeded in bringing about wage restraint and was close to this kind of "bargain".

The Relevance of Keynesianism: Union-Voluntary Unemployment

In my presidential address, I analysed various theoretical models, includ-ing Keynes' own model in *The General Theory*, to see where wages fitted in. The main point is that I became an advocate of wage restraint for the sake of improving employment but also bearing in mind that the employment problem was focussed primarily on the youth labour market. I argued, rather undiplomatically, that the trade unions, with their pressure for increasing wages, caused unemployment, and insofar as they knew what they were doing (there was rational expectations), unemployment was "union voluntary". Some unemployment, of course, was "private voluntary".

In later years—the period of my retirement 2003–2016—I believed that orthodox Keynesian policies were, at various times, highly appropriate. This was particularly true in 2008, when the Global Financial Crisis hit the world, and the Labor Rudd government did follow a deliberate Keynesian fiscal expansionary policy. Excessive wage growth was not a problem. This more recent situation contrasted with the earlier post-Whitlam period I am discussing here, beginning in 1974. One's choice of models must depend on circumstances. I believe that John Maynard Keynes would have agreed with me.

Some Dutch Disease History

I now come to another topic which occupied me. This is the Dutch Disease. This term is usually used for the adverse by-products of an export boom and was invented by *The Economist* magazine in 1977. It referred to the adverse effects of the Dutch natural gas discoveries in the North Sea on Dutch manufacturing in the 1960s. Hence this whole vast literature comes now under the title "Dutch Disease". One sector of an economy is better off because of a boom in its income, and this causes another sector to be worse off. In the British case, the real appreciation of the pound sterling owing to the discovery of oil in the North Sea reduced the international competitiveness of its manufacturing industries. There were gainers and losers. Often one is asked: Why should a rise in income be a "disease"? Answer: it is a "disease" from the point of view of the loser.

Many countries had such oil booms as a result of the big oil-price rises, and many more countries had booms of this kind in the past, whether caused by oil (Norway), other natural resources (Chile,) or indeed a variety of causes including financial booms (Switzerland). Such booms were indeed not new to Australia. In 1859, the British economist Cairnes wrote about the effects of the Australian boom caused by gold discoveries. More recently, Australia had an export boom in the 1970s, and this led to an influential literature, where professors Bob Gregory and Richard Snape analysed the domestic economic implications, and indeed anticipated key themes of the new literature. The issue that Gregory raised and Snape elaborated was widely known in Australia as the Gregory Problem. It was the adverse by-product on Australian manufacturing industries through real appreciation of a boom now known as the Dutch Disease. Two economists—Forsyth and Kay (Forsyth being an Australian)—notably also drew on this Australian experience in discussing the British case with an article entitled "The Economic Implications of North Sea Oil Revenues".

My own survey article "Booming Sector and Dutch Disease Economics: Survey and Consolidation" (1984) was written at the ANU in my second period there. In this article, I have listed many of these earlier contributions, as well as a large number of more recent publications by numerous authors worldwide. In fact, a new field of study has growth up quite rapidly, built on earlier writings but essentially stimulated by the oil shocks of the 1970s and 1980s. The central theme was that a boom, which had a favourable effect on one part of the economy, was likely under particular circumstances to have an unfavourable effect on another part. From 1981 to 1984, I published six articles in this field. By far the most cited, and thus influential, article was the one written jointly with Peter Neary.

The Corden-Neary Article

I visited Oxford in 1979, and that was when Peter Neary and I conceived our joint paper, "Booming Sector and de-Industrialisation in a Small Open Economy". Peter was a former student of mine in Oxford, and at the time we wrote our article, he was a research fellow of Nuffield College. He is now (2016) a professor at Oxford and president-elect of the Royal Economic Society. Not only for me but also for him, it has been the most cited paper. Our joint article is pretty complicated because it considers many possible models, and it also shows clearly possible boom effects on factor incomes and especially on wages. Peter provided all the mathematics, including an impressive Mathematical Appendix. This paper is widely referred to and studied because the Dutch Disease problem appears at various times in many countries and is seen as a serious problem. This was a very successful collaboration between two complementary academics.

In terms of citations, this article has been very successful. But there has been one article produced in the department which has outshone it. In 1964, I visited the University of Chicago and met Herbert Grubel, a rising star who became one of my closest friends. I arranged for him to visit the department, which he did in 1969. But by the time he arrived, I had left for Oxford. He then collaborated with Peter Lloyd (who had recently arrived in the department) to write *Intra-Industry Trade: The Theory and Measurement of International Trade in Differentiated Products* (1975), which became a very influential book and received even more citations than the Corden-Neary article.

On Being a Travelling International Economist

After 20 years writing books and articles some of which have been widely read, at least in the international economics profession, it is not surprising that I received and accepted numerous invitations from around the world to give talks, present papers at conferences, and so on. This was particularly so in this period since my writings on protection and, even more so, on international monetary issues were highly topical.

This also meant that I received many requests from journal editors for refereeing submitted articles. In general, I tried to be constructive in my referee reports. This took a lot of time but was the inevitable duty of someone in my position. Here I shall write a bit more about the particularly attractive benefit of my reputation, namely through travelling.

In 1982, I went, with Dorothy, for nearly two months to Stockholm at the invitation of the Institute for International Economic Studies. I gave a seminar on "The Logic of the International Monetary Non-System" which I later incorporated in a third edition of my book *Inflation, Exchange Rates and the World Economy*. The institute was impressive in the quality of its staff, visitors, and output. It specialised in getting a flow of prominent international visitors. It showed what could be achieved in a "peripheral" country. Its transformation was due to one person, namely Assar Lindbeck, a (or the) leading Swedish economist, who was director of the institute for many years. It gave me an idea of what the department at ANU could achieve. But I realised that I did not have the forceful personality of Lindbeck to bring about the necessary changes. Later, I became a member of the advisory board of the institute.

Here I might immodestly mention that in 1976 (when I was still based in Oxford), I had visited Stockholm for the Nobel Symposium in honour of Bertil Ohlin, a superstar of the economics profession, who had written his most influential publications, notably *Interregional and International Trade*, in the 1930s. He had retired from Swedish politics and was returning to the academic world. I have a photo of Ohlin and me, and he told me that he had read and appreciated my "Recent Developments in the Theory of International Trade" (written at the ANU!), which had helped him to catch up with the field to which he had made such notable contributions in the 1930s.

In 1983, I spent some time at the European University Institute, located on a hill just outside Florence, a visit that greatly appealed to Dorothy. We stayed in the heart of Florence, opposite the Pitti Palace. I gave a variety of lectures to students at the institute, but the main byproduct was that I was invited to the Bologna-Claremont Monetary Conference, which took place at the time in neighbouring Bologna. This conference took place every two years and moved between Bologna and Claremont (California). The last conference was in 1997.

A major event in my life was the invitation to join the Group of Thirty, a highly select group. The 1982 meeting was in Budapest, followed by Toronto, and then Tokyo in 1983. I finally retired from the Group of Thirty in 1990.

In this second ANU period, I also enjoyed visits in 1979 to Seoul and Tokyo (Ford-sponsored seminars, lectures, and the Pacific Trade and Development conference), Paris (OECD), Singapore (1981 and 1982), New Delhi (conference on trade policy), Santiago de Chile (conference on protection), Maui (conference on US-Japan-Southeast Asia relations), and Namur, Belgium (International Trade Conference). Finally, I had an association, involving several visits, during 1978–1980, with the City University, London.

An absolute highlight was the 1984 conference organised by the Federal Reserve Bank at Boston, "Forty Years after Bretton Woods", held in the Mount Washington Hotel, Bretton Woods, New Hampshire. This had a very large number of attendees, including many of my friends— and including also no doubt the less-visible spirit of John Maynard Keynes.

Harry Johnson Dies

In May 1977, I was in Canberra and received a message from Geneva that Harry Johnson had died suddenly at age 53. The Institute for International Economics at the University of Geneva was celebrating its 50th anniversary in 1977 (it was the same age as I was), and Harry was to have been the keynote speaker. Their urgent message was: Would I come in his stead? I did.

Harry Johnson has been a major figure in my life, and indeed a major figure internationally for all my generation in the field of international economics. Many of us owe him a great deal for his support. Hence, it was a really sad occasion. I had earlier written an obituary of Harry for the *London Times*. This was published the next day, to the surprise of some who did not realise that these obituaries are written in advance. Later, I wrote a very thorough review of his "Contributions to International Trade Theory", published in the *Journal of Political Economy* 1984.

Four Notable ANU Professors

Finally, I write here about four ANU professors who not only made an impact in the ANU but also more broadly in Australia and internation-ally. Comprehensive biographies of these four, and indeed many other Australian and New Zealand Economists, can be found in King (ed.) *A Biographical Dictionary of Australian and New Zealand Economists*, and I aim only to supplement these biographies. Primarily I limit myself to my personal contacts and experiences with them. All four have been heads of the ANU economics departments, two in RSSS (social sciences school) and two in RSPAS (Asian and Pacific studies school). Swan was the first head of the RSSS department, followed by Gruen, and Crawford was the first head of the RSPAS Department, followed by Arndt.

Trevor Swan

He was at the ANU during my first ANU period (1962–1967). Like other people I hardly saw him, except that he took me for lunch once at the Commonwealth Club, where he used to meet senior government officials. He acquired justified international fame for his theoretical writings, but his great interest was actually in Australian economic policy. Before he came to the ANU as professor, he had been a very creative public servant—a committed policy adviser.

Now, I have to admit that I fell in love—not with the rather remote Trevor but with a wonderful diagram, the Swan diagram, that he devised as a by-product of an analysis of Australian macroeconomic policy in an unpublished conference paper. I heard about it, when in 1958 I came from London to Melbourne. I then used it for teaching balance of payments theory at the University of Melbourne. At that time only one other person, Heinz Arndt—teaching in a University of Melbourne branch located in Canberra—did the same. In fact, he anticipated me. The essential point is that the Swan diagram integrated very neatly the two aspects of macroeconomic (or balance of payments) theory, namely aggregate demand, determined by fiscal and monetary policy, and relative costs, determined by exchange rate policy or its alternative, which at that time for Britain and Australia was import restrictions policy, and also wage policy. This integration was actually done famously by Meade in his classic book *The Balance of Payments,* but not with a neat diagram. Meade's work was genuinely pioneering. To some extent, he may have got his ideas from discussions with Keynes, with whom he worked during the war. Peggy Hemming and I working together at the National Institute in London had independently devised a diagram aimed at the UK situation at the time, with import controls, but our diagram lacked neatness.

When I came to the ANU, I integrated the Swan and the Hemming-Corden diagrams and thus produced my own version, which was published internationally as "The Geometric Representation of Policies to Attain Internal and External Balance" (1960), and for a time my article became widely read and cited.

Swan, very oddly, seemed to be reluctant to publish, and his original diagram for a long time was just circulated informally in Australia. It was first published in *The Australian Economy: A Volume of Readings*, edited by Heinz Arndt and me. To include Swan's article was Arndt's excellent idea. Since then, there has been a huge literature in this field, with contributions by Harry Johnson, Rüdiger Dornbusch, and many others. Both the origins of these ideas and the later literature have recently been comprehensively—indeed brilliantly—surveyed in Metaxas and Weber "An Australian Contribution to International Trade Theory: The Dependent Economy Model". *The Economic Record*, September 2016. This article reproduces all the various diagrams.

Apart from teaching, I have expounded and used the Swan diagram in various places, notably in my book *Too Sensational: On the Choice of Exchange Rate Regimes* and in "China's Exchange Rate Policy, its Current Account Surplus and the Global Imbalances". *The Economic Journal,* November 2009.

Swan did much else, but very little that was published. Apart from the Swan diagram, his international reputation rests on his contribution to neoclassical growth theory, where also he produced a highly original diagram. His model and article were done quite independently at about the same time as that by Robert Solow, whose contribution won him a Nobel Prize.

Sir John Crawford

"Yes, Sir John". "Of course, Sir John". "As you say, Sir John". He was a man of authority who got things done. He founded the Research School of Pacific and Asian Studies (RSPAS) of the ANU and was the first head of its Department of Economics. He appointed me to this department in 1962. He was a creator of institutions that lasted, and a person with national and international influence. He filled me with awe. Here is a list of just *some* of his successful activities.

At the international level, there was the work he did through his chairmanship of the Technical Advisory Committee of the Consultative Group on International Agricultural Research (CGIAR). This organisation sponsored numerous agricultural research institutes around the world. Basically, it was concerned with the world food problem. For details on all these topics, see various essays in Evans and Miller (eds) *Policy and Practice: Essays in Honour of Sir John Crawford.*

In Australia, he had many achievements. Ross Garnaut's essay about him in the biographical book by King (ed) gives details. He was head (Secretary) of the Federal Department of Commerce and Agriculture when the pioneering Australia-Japan Trade Agreement was reached; first director of the Bureau of Agricultural and Resource Economics; first chairman of the board of trustees and initiator in 1980 of the Australian Centre for International Agricultural Research which sponsored research benefiting developing countries; and initiator and deputy chairman of the Vernon Committee of Inquiry into the Australian economy.

In my view, his most important contribution ever was his work on Indian agriculture, where he was a consultant working in collaboration with the World Bank. He was highly influential in bringing the Green Revolution to India. He led the Agricultural Section of the World Bank Mission (the Bell Mission) to India in 1964–1965 and again in 1967. The background is that Indian agricultural output had not been keeping up with population growth, and this indeed was India's most important economic problem. Sir John recommended policies that were indeed adopted and eventually did succeed in greatly increasing agricultural output in India. From 1973 to 1980, he visited India every year. He was very practically minded, and also persuasive. He knew how to convert policy into practice. The details of his proposals are quite fascinating.

Like many people who came into contact with Sir John, and especially Indians, I have a huge admiration for him. Perhaps he was one of the world's most useful economists! I recommend a book of essays in his honour by Evans and Miller (eds.), *Policy and Practice: Essays in Honour of Sir John Crawford.* An essay by David Hopper describes Sir John's s work on agriculture in India in detail.

I have one specific recollection about Sir John. As mentioned above, he had been the moving spirit in creating the Vernon Committee to review the Australian economy and was its deputy chairman. Their report made recommendations which the Commonwealth Treasury did not like and indeed lobbied against after the Committee's report was published. Thus, there was a debate. At that crucial time, Sir John was absent from Canberra. I thought at the time that this was very unfortunate and said to myself (without fortunately going public on the matter) that he should not be away at such a crucial time; he should defend the report. In 1984 he died, and there was a moving memorial service in his honour. Dr David Hopper, a Vice President of the World Bank, came from Washington DC especially for this occasion and spoke at length about the great influence that Sir John had in India, and what a tremendous difference he had made to Indian agriculture and hence to the Indian standard of living. I also received such a message at this or possibly another occasion from a senior Indian politician. So, I thought: now I know why Sir John was away from the rather trivial Australian Vernon Committee debate. He was, effectively, saving millions of Indian lives!

Heinz Arndt

When I was at the University of Melbourne (1958–1961) I went to Canberra to attend a conference organised by Heinz Arndt about "import replacement". Heinz and his wife, Ruth, were very hospitable and invited participants to their home for a reception. As I wandered around his house, I noticed a familiar picture on the wall—it showed the medieval town hall of Breslau, the city's landmark. This is how I discovered that he was also a Breslau boy. I should mention that his father was a professor, while mine was just the manager of a store. In Germany, professors have much higher status than managers of stores, and this may explain why our personal styles have been rather different.

Later, when I moved to ANU 1962–1967, we collaborated both in producing *Readings on the Australian Economy*—edited by Arndt and

Corden—and also in writing a survey (really a kind of analytical outline) for the planned Vernon report. Also, he organised a session on *Recent Developments* in various branches of economics as part of an economics conference. This led me to write my *Recent Developments in the Theory of International Trade*, which turned out to make an international impact and played a role in my getting appointed to Oxford later.

Heinz's great achievement at the ANU was to establish and keep going the Indonesia project. Here, let me add some characteristics I have observed about him, which have already been published in *A Conversation with Max Corden* by William Coleman.

Heinz was a very sophisticated, civilised person. He was a very good economist; he had a lot more intuition than most technical economists; he could see through an issue in an argument, and this was very apparent to me not long after getting to know him. He had many virtues. He was a man of high principle, which also meant that he held strong convictions. He was very conscientious—if a student gave him a draft of a chapter, he would read it and comment on it promptly in detail and not in a few words, so he was greatly respected among students. He was 12 years older than me, and when I first came to ANU in 1962, I felt he was the great man and I was just his disciple. We did things together. There are a lot of things to be said in his favour. Of course, my brother Gerald had taught me how to be a younger brother.

Heinz was not a modern economist because he never was as rigorous and explicit as necessary in modern economics. But he was aware of that and felt a sense of inadequacy because of it. Actually, in my view, formed very early, he was better than most modern economists, and I had a great respect for him as an economist, even though becoming more explicit in his arguments—perhaps even with a diagram or two—would have been helpful. Let me also add that for a long time, he was a member of the board of *The Economic Record*, and he gave incredibly thorough comments on submitted papers. I benefited from this way back in 1954 before I had actually met him, when I sent a paper from the LSE to the *Record*. Actually, his great strength was the history of thought, rather than area studies, and after he retired he wrote an excellent book published by the University of Chicago Press, and read worldwide, namely *Economic Development: The History of an Idea*.

Heinz had a varied and interesting life. While quite young in England, he became famous for his book *The Economic Lessons of the Nineteen Thirties*. In Australia his best-known, widely read book was *The Australian Trading Banks*. In addition to his biography in King (ed), there is a more comprehensive biography in Coleman, Cornish, and Drake, *Arndt's Story: The Life of an Australian Economist*.

Fred Gruen

Fred Gruen was my closest friend and intellectual and conversational soulmate at the ANU during my second ANU period, 1977–1986. He had succeeded Trevor Swan as head of the economics department in RSSS. His primary interest was in Australian economic policy, which, of course, overlapped with my interests. His original field was agricultural economics but with the relative decline of agriculture in the Australian economy, he shifted his interests. Notably, he was a key adviser to the Whitlam (Labor) government (1972–1975), working closely with Prime Minister Whitlam. He played the key role in several policy decisions, notably the 25% tariff cut of 1973 and the reintroduction of the asset test on pensions in 1985. He wrote many perceptive articles on Australian economic issues. At the ANU, he founded the influential Centre of Economic Policy Research and organised a major survey of Australian economics writing. He and I only wrote one joint paper, namely "A Tariff that Worsens the Terms of Trade", but this turned out to have significant theoretical impact, mainly thanks to Ron Jones, the leading international trade theorist. The basic idea, borne out of the Australian experience, was Fred's, and my contribution was to formalise it.

Fred was born in Vienna and was 16 when he left Vienna for England without his family. He was 19 when he came to Australia in 1940 as an internee, travelling with a large group of mainly German and Austrian Jews. The name of the ship was *Dunera*, and this group came to be known as the Dunera Boys. They were interned in remote Hay NSW for some time, and later they were released, with some returning to Britain and others (some now well-known, like Fred) becoming Australian citizens.

When Fred died in 1997, there was an outpouring of grief and praise. I don't think I have met anybody in my life whom I have admired so much for his personality and balanced judgement. Many others have reacted in the same way. See especially the tribute to him in Bruce Chapman, *The Economic Record*, 1998. I wrote his biography in King *(ed)*. Also, there is "Fred Gruen: A Celebration of his Life", published by the ANU (1997), which includes a short autobiography. His early life has some similarities with my life, but his luck came somewhat later in his life. Like me he married a "local girl". Their two sons have both become influential Australian economists.

Harvard

At the end of this ANU period, in 1986, I occupied the Australian Studies Chair at Harvard for six months. It was a very good experience. I taught a (small) class on the economics of small, open economies, including, of course, Australia but also some Latin American countries. Dorothy and I were based at Winthrop House, and we enjoyed our contacts with the students. I gave a talk about Australia to them. Barry Eichengreen, then a junior member of the faculty, was very helpful. I got to know him and Richard Caves well, and some others, notably Richard Cooper, whom I knew from London days. We travelled in New England, sometimes with Barry.

After Harvard, we were due to spend some time in Kiel, at the *Institut für Weltwirtschaft,* where I would be awarded the 1986 Bernhard Harms Prize and also participate in a symposium, where I was to present the opening paper. Hence while at Harvard, I prepared two papers:

"Fiscal Policies, Current Accounts and Real Exchange Rates: In Search of a Logic of International Policy Coordination" (Harms lecture)
"Why Trade is Not Free: Is there a Clash Between Theory and Practice?" (Symposium)

When I delivered my Harms Prize lecture in Kiel, I started it in German but then switched to the main lecture in English.

What Happened to the Department When I Left?

From October 1986 to end 1988, I was on leave from the ANU to work at the International Monetary Fund (IMF) in Washington DC. While there I was offered a position at the School of Advanced International Studies of the Johns Hopkins University (SAIS), which I accepted. Thus, I resigned from the ANU at the end of 1988. Ross Garnaut then succeeded me as head of the Department. He remained Head for 11 years.

He had been a member of the department while I was head, but he was on leave for six years to act as Economic Adviser to the Prime Minister (Bob Hawke) and then as Ambassador to China. In both positions, he was an outstanding success. Notably, as adviser to the Prime Minister he played a key role in Australia's exceptional tariff reform process at that time. My earlier writings also, of course, played a role, but it was crucial that Ross had the complete confidence of the Prime Minister.

Ross was highly qualified for the department head position, being an excellent economist with a strong interest in policy but also with experience of and interest in the Asia region. Earlier, he had been an adviser to the Government of Papua New Guinea (PNG) and also spent time with the ANU's PNG Research Unit. When he came back to the Department in 1989, he wrote a study entitled "*Australia and the Northeast Asian Ascendancy*", which subsequently influenced the Australian government's policy towards Asian countries. Later, he developed much-needed work on the Chinese economy, in collaboration with others at the ANU, notably Peter Drysdale (whom I supervised as a PhD student when I was at the ANU 1962–1967). As a result of Ross' initiative, for a period the department had an excellent group of PhD students from China, who added to the strength of the student body.

In 2007—long after I had left the ANU, and Heinz had died—the name of the department was changed to the *Arndt-Corden Department of Economics*. It seems that both Heinz and I had left our marks, but in different ways. But I must confess that if Ross had not been away, working for the PM, probably he would have been head of the department in the period 1980–1986 instead of me, which (selfishly) would have suited me and been good for the department—but would have been a serious loss for the prime minister and thus Australia.

Bibliography

WM Corden, "The Geometric Representation of Policies to attain Internal and External Balance", *Review of Economic Studies*, 1960.

Arndt, HW and WM Corden (eds.) The Australian Economy: A Volume of Readings, Cheshire 1963.

Arndt, HW, *The Australian Trading Banks*, Cheshire 1957.

Arndt, HW, *Economic Lessons of the Nineteen Thirties*, Royal Institute of International Affairs, 1963.

Swan, T, *"Longer Run Problems of the Balance of Payments" (1955), in* Arndt, HW and WM Corden (eds.) *The Australian Economy: A Volume of Readings,* Cheshire *1963.*

WM Corden, with Fred Gruen, "A Tariff that Worsens the Terms of Trade", Studies in International Economics, 1970.

WM Corden, "Wages and Unemployment in Australia", *The Economic Record,* 1979.

WM Corden, "The NIEO Proposals: A Cool Look." *Thames Essay* 21, 1979.

WM Corden with Peter Dixon "A Tax-Wage Bargain: Is a Free Lunch Possible?" *The Economic Record*, 1980.

WM Corden, "The Exchange Rate, Monetary Policy and North Sea Oil; The Economic Theory of the Squeeze on Tradeables." *Oxford Economic Papers,* 1981.

WM Corden with Peter Warr, "The Petroleum Boom and Exchange Rate Policy in Indonesia". *Ekonomi dan Keuangan Indonesia,* 1981.

WM Corden, "Exchange Rate Policy and the Resources Boom", *The Economic Record,* 1982.

WM Corden, with Peter Neary, "Booming Sector and De-Industrialisation in a Small Open Economy", *The Economic Journal,* 1982.

WM Corden, "Reflections on Japan in the World Economy", *Look Japan,* 1983.

WM Corden, "Macroeconomic Targets and Instruments for a small Open Economy". *Singapore Economic Review,* 1984.

WM Corden, "Harry Johnson's Contributions to International Trade Theory", *Journal of Political Economy,* 1984.

WM Corden, "Booming Sector and Dutch Disease Economics: Survey and Consolidation, *Oxford Economic Papers,* 1984.

WM Corden, "Fiscal Policies, Current Accounts and Real Exchange Rates: In Search of a Logic of International Policy Coordination", Weltwirtschaftliches Archiv, 1986.

WM Corden, "Why Trade is not free. Is there a Clash between Theory and Practice?" *Weltwirtschaftliches Archiv*, 1987.

WM Corden, "China's Exchange Rate Policy, its Current Account Surplus, and the Global Imbalances"' *The Economic Journal* 2009.

Cairnes, JE, *The Australian Episode* 1859.

Arndt, HW, *Economic Development: The History of an Idea*, Chicago University Press, 1987.

Evans, LT and J D P Miller (eds.) *Policy and Practice: Essays in Honour of Sir John Crawford* Australian National University Press 1987.

Forsyth, P, and John Kay, "The Economic Implications of North Sea Oil Revenues", 1980.

Garnaut, Ross, *Australia and the Northeast Asian Ascendency*, Australian Government Publishing Service, Canberra, 1989.

Grubel, Herbert and Peter Lloyd, *Intra-Industry Trade: The Theory and Measurement of International Trade in Differentiated Products,* Macmillan, 1975.

Gregory RG, "Some Implications of the Growth of the Mineral Sector", *Australian Journal of Agricultural Economics*, 1976

Snape R, " Effect of Mineral Developments on the Economy", *Australian Journal of Agricultural Economics,* 1977

King JE, *A Biographical Dictionary of Australian and New Zealand Economists*, Edward Elgar 2007

Coleman, Peter, Selwyn Cornish and Peter Drake, *Arndt's Story: The Life of an Australian economist,* Asia-Pacific 2007.

Metaxas, E and Ernst Weber, "An Australian Contribution to International Trade Theory; The Dependent Economy Model". *The Economic Record* 2016.

Hill, Hal, *The Indonesian Economy*, Cambridge University Press 1996.

15

International Monetary Fund

In October 1986, I took up a new temporary position (two years and three months) as senior adviser in the research department of the IMF (known as the Fund). I pioneered that position, and various well-known academics succeeded me. The offer to me by the Fund was influenced by various articles I had written on international monetary issues. But my reputation was dominated by "protection", so, as soon as I came to the Fund, I was asked to do a Board Paper on protection. A "Board Paper" was one that was presented at a meeting of the Executive Board, which consisted of representatives of the member-countries as well as some members of the staff. Such a paper was circulated throughout the Fund for reviews and comments before being circulated for discussion at the Board. This paper, entitled "Protection and Liberalisation: A Review of Analytical Issues" was later published and had wide circulation and readership.

The hot, current issues then at the Fund were neither about protection nor about the international monetary system that I had written about before I came but rather about the Latin American debt crisis and the closely related proposals for debt relief.

© The Author(s) 2017
W.M. Corden, *Lucky Boy in the Lucky Country*, Palgrave Studies in the History of Economic Thought, DOI 10.1007/978-3-319-65166-8_15

The Latin American Debt Crisis

Between 1973 and 1982, Latin American governments and their agencies borrowed heavily from private banks, especially the big international ones, and these banks financed their loans through an influx of funds from oil-rich countries that had benefited from the steep increases in oil prices. Thus, effectively through the intermediation of the private banks, the oil funds were lent to the Latin American governments and their agencies. This was a case of "recycling". The biggest borrowers were Brazil, Mexico, Chile, and Argentina, though there were also many others. In the case of Mexico, these borrowed funds actually supplemented its spending of its own gains from its recently discovered oil resources. Its spending increased in the expectation of big gains. There had been a fear that the high savings of the oil producers would have a deflationary effect on the world economy, but this was initially avoided (or moderated) by this recycling of the funds by the banks to countries very eager to spend more.

But then (around 1981 and 1982), owing to a change in US monetary policy, world interest rates increased, the world moved into recession, and the net result was that the borrowing countries could not pay back their loans or even pay adequate debt service. Thus, they moved into financial crises—and that, as always, was where the Fund came in. It moved to restructure the debt payments and provide new emergency loans with very strict conditions. The aim of restructuring was to reduce the payments that the governments had to make (or stretch out the period of repayments), something that the banks would naturally not welcome. In return, the indebted governments or their agencies would have to pursue some unpopular policies, such as spending less.

The Fund is like a doctor who enters the story when the patient is exceptionally sick, possibly through his foolish, irresponsible decisions earlier. Indeed, when I came to the Fund at the end of 1986, the patient was suffering from high temperature. When the doctor insists on improved behaviour, his patients begin to dislike him and wonder whether they might not do better by trying another doctor, possibly one who believed in different medical theories. So-called neoclassical economics, involving fiscal budget tightening and structural reforms to free up labour and product markets, became unpopular in Latin America under the title of "The Washington Consensus".

An International Debt Facility?

By the time I came to the Fund and settled down, I realised that "debt relief" or "reconstruction" was the big issue. The official policy of the USA (and hence the Fund) was that the indebted countries and the international banks need to negotiate and come to debt relief agreements, possibly with the help of the Fund giving guidance about necessary domestic-policy changes. But it was not the policy that either the USA or the Fund (or indeed the World Bank) would provide long-term, large-scale financial assistance. The Fund should continue to provide only short-term macroeconomic crisis loans, as it had been doing for many years and for many countries. At the same time, the World Bank might provide long-term loans for particular projects.

At the same time, many individuals from outside the Fund (e.g. professors Peter Kenen and Jeffrey Sachs) did make more radical proposals for an international debt facility. This would buy the debt of developing countries at a discount and then mark down its contractual value. That would solve the big problem and put an end to the crisis. But how would that affect the debtor countries, the creditor banks, and the owners of the facility? Surely the countries and the banks would welcome it, but the costs would probably be borne by the owners of the facility. The owners might be the IMF or the World Bank, or one or more of the major non-indebted countries, especially the USA. Crucially, a lot would depend on detailed arrangements.

This led me, on my own initiative and without specific authorisation, to make a detailed analysis of a possible international debt facility, focusing on the net gains or losses of various parties, and various detailed arrangements. This analysis was complex, and I cannot summarise it here.

Of course, I realised that, at the time, the establishment of such a facility might or would lead to the Fund or the USA making losses. Hence, it was not then the policy of the Fund or the USA to support such an idea. But my analysis could turn out to be useful if the policy changed. Understandably, the deputy managing director of the Fund decided that my paper should not appear as a Working Paper of the Fund—that is, it should not be seen outside the Fund. The Fund and the US government wanted the indebted countries and the private banks to come to an agreement with each other, without drawing on guarantees of some kind from the Fund or the USA. The latter were the potential third parties and the two interested parties (or groups)—the borrowers and the lenders—should not expect to be rescued by third parties because then they will not make an effort to reach an agreement among themselves. If it came to be known that such an analysis was being carried out at the Fund, the interested parties—the borrowing governments and the lending banks—would have some hope that they would be rescued without having to make sacrifices.

The Brady Plan

This story has an interesting ending.

Policy in this area was not made in the Fund but rather in the US Treasury. And in late 1988 (just before I left the Fund), the Brady Plan was announced, named after the new US secretary of the Treasury. This was a genuine attempt at a radical solution. I will describe it briefly below. As I understand it, the Fund or the USA would not provide guarantees, and thus run risks.

Very soon after the Brady Plan announcement, a message came from the deputy managing director: "Mr Corden can now put his paper into the *Working Paper* series. In fact, it could be published in the Fund's academic-style journal, the *Staff Papers*". Hence, it was indeed published in *Staff Papers* (1988) just as I had written it.

The basic Idea of the Brady Plan was to put an end to the repeated rounds of rescheduling and restructuring of sovereign and private-sector debt in the belief that there was just a temporary liquidity problem. It was believed that the various Latin American countries were no nearer to financial health. The plan required indebted countries individually to engage in negotiations with their commercial bank-creditors.

There were three parts to the story. (1) Bank creditors would grant debt relief in exchange for greater assurance of repayment through principal and interest collateral. (2) There would be some assurance of economic reform. (3) Very important, the resulting debt would be more highly tradable to allow creditors to diversify risk more widely.

I believe that it was successful. The first country to restructure its debt under the plan was Mexico in 1989, and this involved the creation of the first Brady bonds.

Impressions of the Fund

I soon learnt that the main activity of the Fund's staff was to review economies of many countries, some very regularly, and recommend, where necessary, macroeconomic adjustment policies, in effect usually focusing on improvement of the current account and on the reduction of inflation. I had many discussions with various staff members, most of them extremely knowledgeable. This was one way of learning about many countries. On the basis of this I wrote a comprehensive paper entitled "Macroeconomic Adjustment in Developing Countries", which was later published outside the Fund in Maurice Scott and Deepak Lal (eds.) *Public Policy and Economic Development: Essays in Honour of Ian Little* (1990).

I met many of the staff and learnt about many countries. I was very impressed with the quality of the staff, with the efficiency of operations, and, in particular, with the amount of information on individual countries available from internal documents. I don't think I made any difference to anything except that the period educated me about the institution. In the latter part of my time, Jacob Frenkel was director of the department, and my closest associates were deputy directors of the department, Morris Goldstein and Andrew Crockett.

Besides the above, I might mention that one feature of the organisation seemed to be (at the time) a heavy emphasis on confidentiality. One develops that as a habit. And I am sure it was necessary. I still remember Morris Goldstein (a New Yorker) handing me one of these confidential documents and saying, "And when you have finished with it, eat it!"

In retrospect I have asked myself: Have my impressions of the Fund been too favourable? A reliable judgement would have required an in-depth study of particular country cases where there, indeed, have been criticisms. I did not do this while I was at the Fund but did indeed do this much later, during the Asian Crisis in 1998, when I gave a public lecture in Singapore about the crisis. This lecture was published by the Institute of Southeast Asian Studies as *The Asian Crisis: Is there a Way out?* In one chapter, I asked: Do the critics of the IMF have a case? It was a typical pro-and-con situation, but I did think that the critics had a case.

A Festschrift for Max

In 1987, I turned 60. Secretly, behind my back, my very good friend Henryk Kierzkowski had organised and edited a Festschrift in my honour, entitled *Protection and Competition in International Trade*. A special function in Washington DC was arranged by Richard Snape. Many friends and stars of international economics contributed. Of course, this had nothing to with the IMF. Thank you, everyone!

Contributors: Henryk Kierzkowski, Alan Deardorff, Richard Brecher, Jagdish Bhagwati, Alasdair Smith, Richard Caves, Ron Jones, Peter Neary, Frances Ruane, Wilfred Ethier, Avinash Dixit, Paul Krugman, Rod Falvey, Ron Findlay, Anne Krueger, Bob Baldwin, and Richard Snape.

Bibliography

Henryk Kierzkowski (ed.) *Protection and Competition in International Trade: Essays in Honor of W. M. Corden*, Basil Blackwell, Oxford 1987

WM Corden, "An International Debt Facility?" *Staff Papers*. International Monetary Fund, vol. 35 September 1988

WM Corden, "Macroeconomic Adjustment in Developing Countries", in *Public Policy and Economic Development*: Essays in Honour of Ian Little, Maurice Scott and Deepak Lal (eds.) Clarendon Press, Oxford 1990.

WM Corden, "The Asian Crisis. Is there a Way Out?" *Institute of Southeast Asian Studies*, Singapore, 1999.

16

Johns Hopkins: Thirteen Years in Washington DC

To SAIS for 13 Years: The Offer and the Decision

I go back to mid-1988. Dorothy and I were living in Washington DC. I had a temporary position as senior adviser with the International Monetary Fund. Our intention was to return to the ANU at the end of 1988 until I finally retired in 1992 at the age of 65. I would thus have another four years at the ANU.

And then Jim Riedel, Professor of International Economics at the School of Advanced International Studies (SAIS) of the Johns Hopkins University, located in Massachusetts Avenue in the heart of Washington DC, came into the picture. SAIS had a professorial economics vacancy that they were in the process of filling. Jim was the chairman of the search committee. He happened to be talking about it to me. I happened to say, "That is a fine position, right in the heart of Washington". I did not think of myself for that position at all. The idea of making yet another permanent move, having moved back and forth between England and Australia twice already, did not enter my mind. After a few days, Jim came back to me, "Max, would you be interested?" "Think about it". I thought, "Not another big move between countries, surely".

© The Author(s) 2017
W.M. Corden, *Lucky Boy in the Lucky Country*, Palgrave Studies in the History of Economic Thought, DOI 10.1007/978-3-319-65166-8_16

I went home and here was my gypsy wife. "Take it, take it!" Dorothy just loved Washington DC—the Smithonian, the National Gallery, the Kennedy Center, and much else. To be brief, Jim and Dorothy together persuaded me. I was indeed reluctant at first. Looking back, it would have been utter madness to say no. The new position suited me fantastically. Some of the benefits I did not anticipate. All I could see was the beauty of the location—centrally located (near Dupont Circle) in a most exciting city and the fact that it was a public-policy school with the kind of students to whom my interest in policy at that stage of my life was thoroughly suited.

This was a turning point indeed. At 62, when many people retire, I took up a position that I held, unexpectedly, for 13 years.

I cannot think of a single negative aspect. Let me list some of the positives. First, there was a happy wife, highly stimulated by what Washington DC had to offer and the many interesting people, mostly international, whom we met and were friends with. Second, I was going back to teaching, which was my comparative advantage and enjoyable for me. Thirdly, there was the continuous stimulus of Washington DC, and especially the proximity of the IMF and the World Bank. And it was a beautiful city, at least the parts that we lived and moved in.

Teaching at SAIS

My main, indeed only, SAIS responsibility was to teach.

1. First there was an early morning, large class, once a week, on the international monetary system. This was heavily policy oriented. I taught basic theory and then covered history and current issues. It was very popular! There were about 100 in the class. I used my own book— *Inflation, Exchange Rates, and the World Economy*—and others. I dealt extensively with current issues, notably the ongoing Mexican crisis, and later the Asian crisis, and international debates about the role of the US economy in the world.

2. Secondly, there was a small graduate-level advanced class on international monetary theory. This was suitable for those wanting to pursue

more economics. It was almost a seminar with student participation (about 15 students)—and was meant to be challenging.

For the large class, I had teaching assistants (TAs). Some were excellent graduate or advanced students, who were very committed to economics. For the whole 13-year period, I had 22 TAs. I have a full list. They were excellent, both personally and in their work. Two of the best were Jaume Ventura, who later studied at Harvard and then held a faculty position at MIT, and Francesco Mongelli with whom I have stayed in close touch while he was (and is) on the staff of the European Central Bank.

Every year, SAIS students choose teachers (by voting) to be awarded the Excellence in Teaching Award. I received this four times, particularly in the early years—1990, 1991, 1994, and 2000. Two of them were shared. My teaching was enjoyable and was appreciated by the students. Many of the students were personable and had broad interests, which was appealing to me. I would guess that at least 50% and possibly more were foreign (non-US). Examining was a bit of a burden, but the TAs did much of it.

After returning to Australia, I maintained contact with a number of these students, mainly those who continued with the study of economics. Any of them who read this now, "Greetings! How are you?"

Other Aspects of SAIS

There were some very interesting members of the faculty, not economists. I note particularly Paul Wolfowitz and Fouad Ajami.

Paul Wolfowitz

Paul was the dean in the latter part of my period there. He had held senior positions in the previous Republican administration (Ambassador to Indonesia, among others) and was influential in the then Bush administration. He had been a leading (perhaps *the* leading) advocate of initiating the war in Iraq. He was a "neoconservative". Apparently, he carried weight with the president.

I found him to be pleasant personally, modest in manner, open to hear different views, and with a manner that one does not expect from right-wing fanatics. He treated me with great respect.

Thus, my impression was highly favourable, even though I did think that the second war of choice against Iraq was unwise. It was particularly unwise because it diverted attention and resources from Afghanistan.

Here I shall just add a personal thought. I was a student at the University of Melbourne during 1946–1949, that is immediately after the war. Many students were veterans (ex-servicemen), thus older than people like me who came straight from school. Among the older students were a number of very active communists, strong believers (I was a social democrat). Some of the communists seemed very pleasant, somewhat intellectual, and quite reasonable. It seemed they were dedicated to improving society. But I thought they were naive. Now here is my point. Paul Wolfowitz reminded me of them—well meaning, intelligent, pleasant in manner, but, arguably, naive. I suppose that naiveté does not go well with power!

I make this comment with hindsight, which is always easy. I believe that Paul held the strong, and understandable, view that Saddam Hussein of Iraq was an evil ruler, and that was indeed correct, and motivated him. But this does raise further questions. Why overthrow this particular evil ruler, and not others? In this particular case, the answer depended on the likelihood of a ruler having available weapons of mass destruction.

The Extraordinary Ajami

Fouad Ajami dominated discussion at the SAIS faculty board. He loved talking and was a master of the English language. One might describe his talk as flowery. But he was a real intellectual, even though he was not a good listener. He also was a neoconservative, who favoured the Iraq "war of choice". We greatly respected each other.

Upon reflection and with hindsight, it has occurred to me that he failed to foresee the problems that did arise in Iraq in spite of his specialised knowledge on the Middle East. He was a Lebanese-born Shia himself and certainly knew all about the Sunni-Shia conflict, but before the war, I never heard him mention the relevance of this issue. When the disastrous war was on the way (and I had already left SAIS), I believe he realised the disaster that had happened. The war took power from the Sunnis and gave it to the Shias (through the democratic process), but the latter misused it. In discussions, I never heard him even to refer to the Sunni-Shia issue, which was the essential reason that the whole ambitious project failed.

In 2011, long after I left SAIS, Fouad left SAIS for Stanford (for the Hoover Institution) and sadly died soon after, at age 68.

Any Problems at SAIS?

The economists, both tenured and non-tenured, were all easy to get on with, and I did not have to do any administration or fundraising. Indeed, I also found the other faculty members (in international relations and area studies) both interesting and agreeable. Did SAIS as an institution have any problems? Its location was fantastic. This meant that leading public figures were happy to come and speak at SAIS. I have personally met some of them, including the Dalai Lama and Hillary Clinton. SAIS seemed to have enough money, and some non-economic faculty members were skilled at fundraising. It did not seem to me that SAIS had any problems.

Finally, I was there just when the debate about starting a war of choice in Iraq was active. I vividly remember Senator Edward Kennedy talking to a large crowd of mainly students at SAIS just a few days before the war started, and I was due to leave. This was an example of the outstanding persons who came to speak at SAIS. He was convincing: Why not wait until the evidence about weapons of mass destruction became clearer?

My Extra Activities at SAIS

I gave various talks and participated in various activities at SAIS. These were lectures, panels about current issues, seminars, and round tables. They were additional to my regular classes. Here is a list of some of the topics:

Sturc lecture 1998: Sense and Nonsense on the Asian Crisis.
Special panel 1998 with Paul Wolfowitz: Indonesia in Crisis

Special lecture 1998: Currency Board and Indonesia
Launch of Soros Book 1998
The Meltzer Commission Recommendation 2000 Panel
Evening seminar 1997: Reconciling Macroeconomic Adjustment with
    Microeconomic reforms
Washington Roundtable 1990: The Future of the International Economic
    System

The World Bank Project

In this period, by far the most important and demanding work for
me was the World Bank project which led to *Boom, Crisis and
Adjustment* (BCA), a huge book (over 400 pages) written jointly with
Ian Little (the leader and initiator), Richard Cooper, and Sarath
Rajapatirana. It involved the study of the macroeconomic policies
and experiences of 18 developing countries. Little (1999, pp. 90–92)
has information on the origin of the project and its teething problems. Essentially it was inspired by Ian's success with an earlier mul-
ticountry project leading to *Industry and Trade in Some Developing
Countries.* Sarath was a staff member of the World Bank and as such
was the director of the project. One by-product of the project was
that Sarath, who, like me, lived in Washington DC, became my close
friend. In fact, he had been my student when I taught at the University
of Minnesota in 1971. Richard Cooper had been my friend since the
LSE days, and Ian Little, of course, had been a close colleague at
Nuffield College.

I was responsible for chapters 6, 7 and 8 of *BCA*. These dealt with
inflation, involving macroeconomic policy in general, and exchange rate
policies. Much of it was recent economic history, and one had to know
about all the 18 countries. I worked on it while I was at the IMF, but for
four years from 1989, I combined teaching at SAIS with absorbing part-
time work at the World Bank. Comparative macroeconomics became my
"field".

There is a negative and a positive side to this project. Let me begin with
the negative side.

How does one analyse the behaviour of 18 countries? One approach would be to add up the data about various countries, giving countries weights of some kind, based perhaps on population or the size of the economy. But that would obscure the differences, and the aim presumably is to learn from their differences, or to understand why they differ. But if you don't add them in some way, you might end with no clear conclusions. The way out is then to add them up in groups—say oil exporters and oil importers, and so on. This actually is what we authors have done in this book. But then no clear answers may emerge.

I was allocated the topic of inflation. A cursory review, after much time spent studying all the 18 countries, led me to conclude that 18 countries were too much to do properly. I then made a wise decision, namely to pick out the six countries that had episodes of very high inflation, and that were also fairly large countries, and put them all into my Chapter 7 of BCA. All the other 12, with moderate inflation, would go into Chapter 6.

For both chapters I made the distinction between *seigniorage inflation, adjustment inflation,* and *spiral inflation,* the first being the most common and well-known. Fiscal deficits are often financed by money creation, and continuous money creation is often the principal cause of inflation. The resultant seigniorage is a form of revenue for the government. *Adjustment inflation* explains short-term inflationary bubbles. An adjustment process may require relative prices changing—for example, the prices of tradables relative to non-tradables, or the prices of exports relative to imports—and this could, in principle, be brought about by some prices (including wages) falling or by other prices rising. But prices and wages are frequently inflexible downwards, so the adjustment is brought about mostly by prices rising. *Spiral inflation* represents a process where higher prices lead to higher wages, hence higher costs, higher prices of non-tradables, further wage increases, and so on. A deterioration of the terms of trade may start off this process, but such a process can only continue if the money supply is steadily increased.

Chapter 7 of BCA—dealing with the six high-inflation countries, namely Brazil, Argentina, Chile, Mexico, Turkey and Indonesia—turned out to be my best and most interesting chapter. For example, in the case of Brazil, I give a systematic account for the whole of 1960–1989 of well-defined periods, and answering simple and obvious questions. I wish this chapter had been published as a separate book, or alternatively my Brazilian section, would have fitted well as part of an economic history of Brazil. And that applies to the five other stories in that chapter.

In my SAIS teaching, as well as lectures outside SAIS, this Chapter 7 of BCA has been very useful. I have had a particular interest in three countries—Argentina, Mexico, and Indonesia—and used them as case studies in my teaching and other writing. Argentina is of interest because it has so many similarities with Australia, and yet since the end of the nineteenth century, Australia has done so much better. Why was that? Mexico, in my time at the IMF and then at SAIS, has had continuing problems and has been prominently in the news. I referred to it a great deal in my SAIS classes. Finally, my interest in Indonesia goes back to my ANU days but also became prominent with the Asian crisis while I was at SAIS.

From my personal point of view, the positive side of the project is that it gave me the knowledge and the foundations for much writing and lecturing that I did in the subsequent period, that is from 1992 to 2000. The study of the 18 countries gave me so much detailed knowledge of their histories and politics that I felt I became as qualified to talk and write about these countries as an experienced much-travelled staff member of the World Bank or the IMF.

I published a number of articles on exchange rate policy—especially one article, "Exchange Rate Policies for Developing Countries", *Economic Journal* (1993)—that all rested on the knowledge I acquired on this project. My last book *Too Sensational: On the Choice of Exchange Rate regimes* (2002) also rested on this foundation.

One should not expect studies of 18 countries to yield simple conclusions or radical new theories. In this respect Sarath's Chapter 9 of BCA on "Trade Policies: Tightening and Liberalization" is a special case. He uncovered something important that had not been noted before, as far as I know, namely the shift towards "The New Liberalization" (p. 271 of BCA). Before the 1980s, it was normal for a balance of payments crisis to lead to the imposition or a tightening of import restrictions. In the 1980s, it became more normal for a balance of payments crisis to lead to (or be associated with) the opposite, namely trade liberalisation. The explanation was that in the 1980s a balance of payments crisis would lead the IMF to come to the rescue and, at the same time, to require trade liberalisation as part of the rescue process essentially for ideological reasons.

Chapter 12 in BCA by Richard Cooper, "The Political Economy of Stabilization and Adjustment", is a tour-de-force that I find fascinating, though it does not, and could not, yield simple unexpected conclusions. It is a crucial chapter because so much of policy changes in the 18 countries can only be explained in political-economy terms.

Conferences: The Great Perk of Academic Life

During the 13 years that I was at SAIS, I received invitations to, and attended, 28 conferences, of which 13 were in mainland USA and 15 elsewhere. One might say that I made my academic reputation at ANU and Oxford and in the SAIS period, I reaped the benefits—since attending conferences was not just enjoyable but getting these invitations was also an indication of my reputation. In addition, the location of SAIS was obviously very convenient for attending all the mainland-located conferences.

Some of the mainland conferences were in honour of long-standing friends and academic colleagues, notably Ron Jones (Rochester), Jagdish Bhagwati (Columbia), Bob Stern (Ann Arbor), and Ronald Findlay (Columbia). The international or overseas conferences were in a great variety of countries or places—Sussex UK, Tokyo, Santander, London, Mexico, La Coruna, Caracas, Potsdam, Konstanz, Honolulu, Paris, and Athens. The Sussex conference was the silver jubilee conference of the International Economics Study Group of which I was one of the founders. A particularly memorable conference—because of the large number attending—was the October 1991 conference at Bretton Woods, which was about a "Retrospective on Bretton Woods". I also have vivid memories of two conferences—1998 and 1999—in Honolulu. Here I express thanks to the many kind hosts of all the conferences.

Lectures or Talks

I gave numerous lectures (or talks) apart from my usual SAIS lectures. There was a great demand because some of the topics on which I had become an expert were highly topical. Of course, the World Bank project gave me much material, but there was also debt relief (on which I had become an expert at the IMF), and the unlimited demand for discussions about trade policy and protection. The international monetary system and the Asian crisis were always hot topics. Essentially, these were all extensions of my teaching career.

I gave 15 lectures at the IMF Institute. Mostly they were on exchange rate theory, regimes and policy, often with case studies. A few were on trade policy. I participated in the Trade Policy Reform Workshop of the World Bank with five lectures. There were 21 lectures that were *not* under the auspices of the IMF or the World Bank—13 of them in the USA and 8 in Europe.

The Group of Thirty

In 1982, when I was at the ANU, I became a member of an organisation called The Group of Thirty. Its correct name was Consultative Group on International Economic and Monetary Affairs, Inc., but the brief title makes it sound almost conspiratorial. Actually, it was a harmless, though interesting, talk-shop on international economic and financial issues. It consisted of current and former heads of many central banks, of the IMF, of the Bank for International Settlements, and also heads of major private banks, and some others. Among the others were a small number of economists both from international institutions and academics. When I joined, there were just two academics, namely the famous (and elderly) Austrian economist, Fritz Machlup, and my old friend from LSE days, Peter Kenen, who was a Princeton professor. On Peter's initiative, I was invited to the group. The group, apart from talking, also published reports which were intended to be forward-thinking.

The group met twice a year in many different places, usually with a local central bank being the host. One annual meeting was usually in New York (hosted by the Federal Reserve Bank of New York) before or after the annual meeting of the IMF.

I stayed in the group until 1990, when I voluntarily retired. Thus, I went to 16 meetings, of which at least eight or more were outside the USA. When I first joined the group, the chairman was Johannes Witteveen, who had been managing director of the IMF. Later chairmen during my membership period were Paul Volcker, former chairman of the Federal Reserve, and Gordon Richardson, former governor of the Bank of England.

During the period that I was a member of the group (the 1980s), there were plenty of international monetary problems, notably the developing countries' (primarily Latin American) debt problem, with which I was concerned when I was at the IMF, and the current account imbalances among developed countries, about which I had also been writing. But some really big problems arose much later, in 2008, with the global financial crisis, and these presented some very important and challenging intellectual issues. By that time, I was no longer a member of the group. It would have been interesting to have been a member then. Perhaps I left the group too early! Of course, I had very quick views on the crisis when it came. See my article entitled boldly "The World Credit Crisis: Understanding It, and What to Do", published in *The World Economy* 2009.

I found formal meetings interesting but, above all, I made very good friends—too many from various countries to list here—who knew more than I did about "real-world" events and how things are done in that world. It was an education for me. I have vivid memories of conversations with individuals while walking in various beautiful environments. I must also add that when bankers have conferences, they are treated to a level of luxury with which academics are not familiar. Only the best hotels will do. And who would not enjoy a conference sponsored by the Banca d'Italia in Venice or Perugia? I owe a lot to the late Peter Kenen, who nominated me to join the Group and has died too young.

The Bologna-Claremont International Monetary Conferences

This conference series was started in 1967 by Randall Hinshaw, professor at Claremont Graduate School (University of Southern California). It met every two years, and moved between Claremont and Bologna, in the latter case based on SAIS-Johns Hopkins Bologna Center. Bob Evans, the director of the centre, was the Bologna organiser. Randall was not only the organiser when the conference was in Claremont but also the fundraiser.

Participation was by invitation for economists (academic and official). There was an open, free-flowing discussion, with just one prepared paper to lead the discussion and define the issues. With such an open discussion, the choice of membership was crucial. Randall made an effort to get top people and especially aimed to get Nobel Prize winners. At these conferences, I met Milton Friedman, Paul Samuelson, James Tobin, Franco Modigliani, and Bob Solow—all Nobel laureates. Other regulars were Bob Mundell (also later a Nobel Laureate), Dick Cooper, and various less well-known, younger people.

I attended three meetings at Bologna and three at Claremont. My first meeting was in 1983 at Bologna. At that time, I was still at the ANU and was visiting Florence (European University Institute), with Dorothy. When Bob Mundell heard that I was nearby, he got me an invitation to Bologna, where the conference had already started. On that occasion, Lionel Robbins (Lord Robbins) was chairman, and James Meade was a participant. Later meetings were chaired by Dick Cooper (another friend from LSE days). In 1997, owing to the late arrival of Cooper, I was asked to chair the meeting. In my notes about this I wrote the following: "I felt like the conductor of a (usually) minor orchestra conducting Yehudi Menuhin, Jascha Heifetz, and other stars. Certainly, it was a major event for me."

These conferences were an opportunity for me to listen to and observe the great Milton Friedman. He was very persuasive and seemingly mild-mannered. He sounded so reasonable. He started with an assumption (which was usually implicit and we might think preposterous) and then logically, everything inevitably followed from that.

I was also struck by the impression I had of some of the famous, elderly participants (i.e. Samuelson, Friedman, Modigliani, and Tobin). They obviously enjoyed themselves, enjoyed discussion, debate for its own sake, and not in order to win. Nothing rude.

The Asian Crisis

I visited Singapore at the invitation of the Institute of Southeast Asian Studies for three weeks in 1998, right in the middle of the Asian crisis. On 6th August, I gave a public lecture to a large audience. The subsequent publication of the lecture was widely read and had to be reprinted. It was entitled "*The Asian Crisis. Is there a Way out?*" Among other things, it examined whether the critics of the IMF had a case (yes, they did), and it had a postscript on Indonesia. It also discussed what lessons could be learnt from the Mexican experience. My basic approach was Keynesian. I asked, "Must such a crisis cause a recession or even a depression?" This is a short booklet which had influence, was topical, and my writing of it benefited from the World Bank project.

Two New Books

In addition to the World Bank project—the product of teamwork—I produced during this period two books of my own. The first was an expansion of the Ohlin lectures which I had given in Stockholm in 2000. Its eccentric title (of the book, not the lectures) was *Too Sensational: On the Choice of Exchange Rate Regimes*. (The title was my choice.)

This book was the major by-product of my work on exchange rate policies for the World Bank project. Its central contribution was that there are three approaches to exchange rate and monetary policy, namely the Nominal Anchor Approach, the Real Targets Approach, and the Exchange Rate Stability Approach. It then related these approaches to three polar exchange rate regimes, namely the Fixed but Adjustable Exchange Rate Regime (FBAR) which is the Bretton Woods system, the

Absolutely Fixed Regime, and the Pure-Floating Regime. To expound the Real Targets Approach it used Trevor Swan's Swan diagram.

It had three chapters on lessons from developing countries: from Argentina—with a separate chapter—from three other Latin American countries, and from seven Asian countries including Hong Kong.

The book received highly favourable reviews by the three leading economists who endorsed it (Barry Eichengreen, Richard Cooper, and Sebastian Edwards) and an enthusiastic and very detailed review by Roberto Rigobon in *The Journal of International Economics,* as well as other favourable reviews in *The Economic Journal, the Journal of Economic Literature, The World Economy*, and the *Southern Economic Journal.*

The other new book entitled *Economic Policy, Exchange Rates and the International System* was originally meant to be a fourth edition of *Inflation, Exchange Rates and the World Economy*, but was much enlarged from this earlier book. It contains much material which I used in my SAIS lectures on the international monetary system.

This new book has an expanded version of a particular chapter from the earlier book, both versions of the chapter being entitled "The International Macro-System". The latest (1994) version is more thorough than the 1986 version and has an Appendix which is supported by a neat diagram (of the kind I like!). I believe that the ideas expounded in this chapter, especially the latest version, are very fundamental and—in my thinking at least—very important. I should have advertised these ideas more vigorously.

Retirement

I retired from SAIS in 2002, at the age of 75. I had been teaching at SAIS for 13 years, which was long enough. Our original plan had been to stay in Washington DC for a few years during my retirement, probably travelling to Europe, especially Oxford. But the situation changed when Dorothy showed signs of developing Alzheimer's. So I decided we must return to Melbourne where family, and especially Dorothy's sister, Ruth, lived.

Bibliography

IMD Little et al. *Boom, Crisis and Adjustment: The Macroeconomic Experience of Developing Countries*, (BCA for short). This was the 400 page fruit of the World Bank project. The authors were IMD Little, Richard N Cooper, WM Corden, and Sarath Rajapatirana. Published by Oxford University Press for the World Bank, 1993.

IMD Little, Collections and Recollections: Economic Papers and their Provenance (This is, in part, autobiographical), Oxford University Press (1999).

WM Corden, Exchange Rate Policies for Developing Countries, *The Economic Journal*, January 1993.

WM Corden, *Economic Policy, Exchange Rates, and the International System*, Oxford University Press and The University of Chicago Press 1994.

WM Corden, *The Asian Crisis. Is there a Way out?* Institute of Southeast Asian Studies, 1999.

WM Corden, *Too Sensational. On the Choice of Exchange Rate Regimes*, MIT Press, 2002.

WM Corden, "*The World Credit Crisis: Understanding It, and What to Do*", *The World Economy*, 2009.

17

Living in Two Countries

Between December 1988 (when I had finished at the IMF) and January 2000, we were living in Washington DC but paid ten visits to Australia. Thus, for the SAIS period we lived in two countries. In all cases, we included visits to Melbourne to spend time with *Mutti* and Mumma (our mothers). Also, I gave many lectures and attended many conferences in Australia. We had kept our house in Canberra and usually split our visits to Australia between Melbourne and Canberra.

In December 1991, I flew to Auckland to attend the wedding of Simon, Gerald's and Peggy's eldest son, while Dorothy flew direct to Melbourne to stay with Mumma.

In our 1992 visit, I attended the Conference of Economists in Melbourne, and in 1993 the conference in Queensland, presenting in the latter case a paper "International Macroeconomic Policy Lessons for Australia" (later published in *The Road to Reform*, Chap. 16). During our 1997 visit, I spent most of my time in Canberra. That was the time when Fred Gruen died, and I wrote his obituary in *The Australian* and also attended two functions in his memory.

© The Author(s) 2017
W.M. Corden, *Lucky Boy in the Lucky Country*, Palgrave Studies in the History of Economic Thought, DOI 10.1007/978-3-319-65166-8_17

Mutti and Mumma Die

Our visit from August 1995 to February 1996 was eventful, with very much sadness but also two honours. Our base was Canberra, but Dorothy spent much of the time in Melbourne.

Mutti died on 21 August 1995 and Mumma in February 1996.

I mentioned earlier in Chap. 12 that my father died at age 62 in 1958. *Mutti* died in 1995 at age 94, so she had been a widow for 37 years.

I should like to say something about these last years of hers and her sisters. She had two sisters, Siddy, who came from Shanghai after the war, and Elli, who lived in England during the war and who played a major role in our lives. She came to Melbourne after her husband died in France. Siddy's husband died in 1966. So there were now three sisters, all widows, in Melbourne.

They all lived in a suburb of Melbourne, Caulfield North, in separate apartments and buildings but within walking distance of each other. They lived independent lives, but sometimes, perhaps often, they would dine together. I did not know Siddy well but can report that Elli, who was very artistic, and actually had painted and also been a photographer, created an elegant European environment for herself, and also had a circle of friends through her contact with the director of Melbourne's National Gallery. She would regularly visit the gallery; in her later years, she was steered around in a wheelchair.

Mutti had different interests. She was very interested in Australian politics, and also world affairs, and loved attending weekly lectures on such matters by Sir Zelman Cowen, when he was a university professor (from 1951 to 1966), lecturing for the Council for Adult Education. Later, he became the governor-general. She was also a great reader. I think I inherited some of her interests and characteristics.

In September 1995, I was awarded an honorary degree from the University of Melbourne, and shortly before that, in August, I went to Adelaide to attend the Conference of Economists, to give my Fisher lecture, and also be awarded the Distinguished Fellowship of the Economic Society. The Fisher lecture was on "Protection and Liberalisation in Australia and abroad" (later published in the *Road to Reform,* Chap. 8).

We also saw Jane during these visits. In 1989, we visited her and John in Forbes, New South Wales, a very attractive, if remote, town, the architecture of which showed that it was once a prosperous gold mining centre. Three years later, in 1992, Jane had left John and moved to another NSW town, namely Narrandera (which was near Forbes), to stay temporarily with a friend. During our visit to Melbourne that year Dorothy and I drove from Melbourne to Narrandera and back, and bought a house for Jane on 3rd June. Fortunately, the decision was easy because there was not much choice. This is also a very attractive town on the Murrumbidgee River. It was once a commercial centre for a prosperous, wheat-growing area.

Gerald Dies

During this last visit to Australia, which ended in January 2000, I had stayed for a while with Gerald and Peggy in Melbourne and had gone for long walks with Gerald. He seemed a little weak. In September 2000, while Dorothy and I were in Oxford and when their son, Martin, was living in London, and I was about to leave for Stockholm to give the Ohlin lecture, we received the news that Gerald had died. This was a big shock. He and I were very close. He would eagerly await my visits to Melbourne and was keen to discuss both economic and political matters with me. His last moments were fortunately completely painless. It was a sudden heart attack.

Peggy told me afterwards that she was aware that this could happen. He was 78 years old. He was an utterly reliable person, in his home life and in his work, with a notable sense of social responsibility. I am proud of the fact that on the Mornington Peninsula (near Melbourne), there are two plaques in his honour, one commemorating his role in organising the improvement of the environment of McCrae Homestead—a historic house belonging to the National Trust—and the other in organising the construction of a community park in the area by the seaside (in Merricks Beach), where his family now has actually three holiday houses. One is the home that Gerald bought in 1968 and Peggy now uses, and where I sometimes stay. The two other houses belong to the families of his two sons, Simon and Martin.

Gerald at School in England

As I noted in Chap. 1, in 1937 Gerald, at age 15, was sent to England to go to Royal Grammar School High Wycombe until December 1938, when he left for Australia with our parents and me. Later, in Melbourne, we gathered that he had fond memories of his English schooldays and, like me he had become an Anglophile. In November 2016, with the help of my Oxford friend, Peter Oppenheimer, I made contact with the school. Louise Bignell, its development and marketing Officer, miraculously found records about him from school lists and the *Old Wycombiensian* magazine

She writes: "From the records I have gleaned, he was certainly a very talented boy and must have worked incredibly hard. His positive attitude must have shone through to give such a good impression on his arrival at RGS." He was there for two terms in 1937 and three terms in 1938. In the latter year, he received the first-form prize for schoolwork. In each term, they list two boys in the form "worthy of praise" for particular subjects, and the records show that he was listed for maths, French, history, physics, Latin, and in one term Scripture.

I am moved and very proud of my big brother.

Ulrich Batzdorf, My School Friend from Breslau

Ulrich Batzdorf (later "Rick" Batzdorf) was my best friend at school in Breslau.

He and his family left Breslau in 1939. He spent a year at a boarding school in England (like me), and then in 1940 he and his family moved to the USA. He and I corresponded regularly between Melbourne and New York in our teen age and college (university) years. Eventually we lost contact.

Years later, I met someone who told me that Rick had moved from New York to Los Angeles (LA). Travelling often between USA and Melbourne, during one of my LA stopovers, I found his name in the LA phone book, and hence made contact. They lived in Santa Monica. After that, Dorothy and I stayed frequently with Rick and his wife, Ellen, during our LA stopovers, and an old friendship was renewed. Rick had met Ellen in England. It is amazing how we four related so easily. Among other things, we seemed to have the same political views. Rick is professor of Neurosurgery at the University of California at Los Angeles (UCLA) Hospital, now (2016) partially retired.

Return to Australia 2002

Dorothy and I returned permanently to Melbourne on 26 October 2002 and moved directly into the Menzies-Malvern, a retirement village— actually an apartment building with independent living—located in the suburb of Malvern. It was named after the former Prime Minister Robert Menzies, who had lived in Malvern after retiring from politics. Malvern is next door to the suburb of Armadale, where Dorothy's sister Ruth lived, and where Dorothy and her siblings had lived when they were children. Indeed, in 1958 Mumma was living in Armadale when Dorothy and I returned to Melbourne from London. In our first year of marriage, we lived there with Mumma.

In January 2001, when I was still in Washington, I was informed by the office of the governor-general of Australia that I had been awarded the Order of Australia and would become a Companion of the Order of Australia (using the label AC), which is the highest level of the Order. I was awarded this "for service as a leading international economist, particularly in the areas of international trade and finance policy development". This was quite an honour for the little immigrant boy from Breslau. I received many letters of congratulations of which I most treasure one from Gough Whitlam AC, former Labor prime minister.

The investiture took place in Melbourne on 26 November 2002, not long after our return from Washington DC. It was in Government House, Melbourne, and the governor-general, Dr Hollingworth, came from Canberra to invest me and two other persons. The family was well-represented with Dorothy, Peggy, Ruth, Simon, Sally (Simon's wife), and Martin. Jane could not come, and it is sad that neither my father, my mother, nor Gerald could be present.

Bibliography

The lectures below are reprinted in WM Corden, *The Road to Reform: Essays on Australian Economic Policy,* Addison, Wesley, Longman, 1997.

WM Corden, "Macroeconomic Policy: Some International Lessons for Australia", *Economic Analysis and Policy,* March 1995.

WM Corden "Protection and Liberalisation in Australia and Abroad" (Fisher Lecture) *Australian Economic Review*, 1996.

18

All About Luck

Have I been a lucky boy? How much of my life has been luck and how much, if any, was planning or good decision-making? Thinking about the early stages—before I became an academic (Part I of this autobiography)—good planning or decision-making by my parents with the support of Aunt Elli was crucial. Thanks to Elli, my brother and I were lucky to arrive in Australia fluent in English. And never to be forgotten, we had plenty of help on the way—from certain Australian politicians and others who ensured that visas were available, the Jewish Welfare Society of Melbourne, and indeed the members of the Jewish community who lobbied in support of such visas. And then there were the kind teachers in my schools. All of this I have described. Essentially, I (with my brother) was a passive recipient of luck. I just had to be on good behaviour and "fit in" in whatever situation I found myself.

Reflecting further on this matter, for our family of four, there was a huge amount of luck compared with so many German Jews who left too late, not to speak of all those Polish Jews who were caught. The first was the lucky effect of a seemingly unlucky event, namely my father losing his job as manager of Trautner (the family firm) in 1937. This directly led to a decision to take immediate steps to make emigration possible and, especially, to

© The Author(s) 2017
W.M. Corden, *Lucky Boy in the Lucky Country*, Palgrave Studies in the History of Economic Thought, DOI 10.1007/978-3-319-65166-8_18

send his sons to England first. Of course, it was too late to actually keep my father out of Buchenwald, but it explained why he was let out fairly soon—because the Australian visa came earlier. The second piece of luck of our family was to have a close, dedicated, and enterprising relative in England, that is Aunt Elli.

And, it is obvious, I was lucky to meet Dorothy. We were well suited, and she enjoyed living in many different places, especially Oxford and Washington DC.

As I write this (in 2016) the world is full of refugees, who are desperate to find a home. That, surely, is a reminder of how lucky we have been.

But what about the academic career? My prospects were completely transformed by getting the British Council scholarship. Thank you, Wilfred Prest, and indeed all my teachers at the commerce faculty of the University of Melbourne. If I had not received the scholarship, I would probably have stayed in the Commonwealth Public Service. I would not have become an academic. I would have been an adequate public servant, conscientious, and good at writing reports, but how would I have been at "office politics" or at dealing with politicians? Who knows? But I am not impressed with my own abilities in that direction. I believe that my strength was and is writing, and that might have benefited my career somewhat.

Beginning with my LSE period from 1953, everything went smoothly. I did not have a high opinion of myself and hence did not have high expectations. This had an advantage: I could be favourably surprised when things went well, as they did after that. Thank you, Britain, for the scholarship and for earlier providing visas for Gerald and me. No wonder we were anglophiles! And thank you, James Meade, the ultimate English gentleman. After that, there were a number of steps, all of which happened without much or any effort on my part. First, getting my first faculty position at the University of Melbourne (thank you, Donald Cochrane), then moving to the ANU which provided a fantastic research environment (thank you, Sir John Crawford), and then perhaps the biggest and least expected step of all, going to Oxford (thank you, many times, Harry Johnson).

Finally, there was the decision to move to SAIS that I have described in detail. Thank you, Jim Riedel and Dorothy.

I did make some key decisions, though not as explicitly as I am writing it down now. It is clear that I am good at teaching. That began early. On the boat from England to Australia I, aged 11, was teaching English to Mr Hecht, an adult family friend from Breslau

My three substantial teaching episodes were at Melbourne (1958–1961), at Oxford (1967–1976), and at SAIS (1989–2002). In the case of Melbourne and Oxford, students have told me years later how they valued my teaching, and in the case of SAIS, it was clear while I was there. Partly I am good at it because I like it, and I like it partly because I have rapport with students. Also, I take teaching seriously, with careful preparation. That is a decision I made. I was conscientious.

I was also good at particular kinds of writing and enjoyed it. Not all economists are as interested in the quality of exposition as I am. Of the three books that I wrote in Oxford, at least two were very well-written— *Trade Policy and Economic Welfare* and *Inflation Exchange Rates and the World Economy*—and reviewers confirmed this. In addition, I was good at writing short, neat theoretical articles, preferably with a simple diagram or two. And I have produced many of these, beginning with the article on newspaper economics.

What decisions did I make? I would concentrate on teaching and on writing, and avoid administrative duties, management of all kinds, and (at SAIS) fundraising. In other words, I would concentrate on what I was best at and avoid what I am probably not so good at. Comparative advantage! Here I made my own luck!

Coming back to the question of luck, some of the invitations to give lectures, to attend stimulating conferences in attractive places, and job offers, or at least suggestions that I should consider certain jobs, were owed to a particular kind of luck. Many people knew me by my expository books and articles, and it is these that lead them to invite me and that benefited my reputation. *And it is just luck that I have this ability at exposition.*

Appendix

Little "Werner" with his "Mutti" in Breslau, at age 6

© The Author(s) 2017
W.M. Corden, *Lucky Boy in the Lucky Country*, Palgrave Studies in the History of
Economic Thought, DOI 10.1007/978-3-319-65166-8

First day at school in Breslau

Little "Werner" in 1938, at age 10

Off to Australia! Departure from Southampton. A historic family picture, December 1938 (From l to r: Vati, Mutti, Aunt Elli (to see us off), Gerhart, and, in front, Werner (later Max). Gerhart was 16 and little Werner 11)

D.M.S. „Sibajak"   N.V. Rotterdamsche Lloyd

The Dutch ship that brought the family from Southampton to Colombo

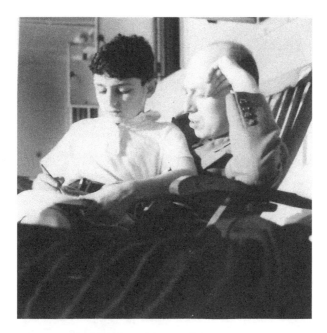

"Werner"on the ship, teaching Mr Hecht English

Mutti and Vati in Australia. They look very young, so probably around 1940

Aunt Elli and Grossmutti in England, during the war, around 1940. Aunt Elli and her husband had wisely emigrated from Berlin to London in 1933. Before the war, they also brought Grossmutti from Berlin

Dorothy and Max in Canberra

Dorothy, Jane, and Max in Canberra

Max in his home office in Oxford

Dorothy, Jane and Max in Oxford or New York

The three sisters in Melbourne. From l to r: Siddy, Elli, Kate (Mutti). Siddy came from Shanghai, Elli from England or France, and Mutti from England. All were born in Breslau, Germany

Dorothy and Max in USA in 2001, before returning to Melbourne

Another historic picture. Max's investiture as Companion of the Order of Australia on 26th November 2002. The Governor-General came from Canberra and it took place in Government House, Melbourne. From l to r Simon, Sally (Simon's wife), Peggy (widow of Gerald), Dorothy, The Governor-General, Dr Hollingworth, Max, Ruth (sister of Dorothy) and Martin. Gerald, my brother, father of Simon and Martin, had died in 2000

Willy Cohn(Uncle Willy). On his way to visiting Palestine 1937. Photo courtesy of Professor Norbert Conrads

Index

© The Author(s) 2017
W.M. Corden, *Lucky Boy in the Lucky Country*, Palgrave Studies in the History of
Economic Thought, DOI 10.1007/978-3-319-65166-8

Printed in Australia
AUOW01n0105190318
295790AU00004B/11